DINOSAURS

THE BIBLE BARNEY & BEYOND

PHIL PHILLIPS

D1367508

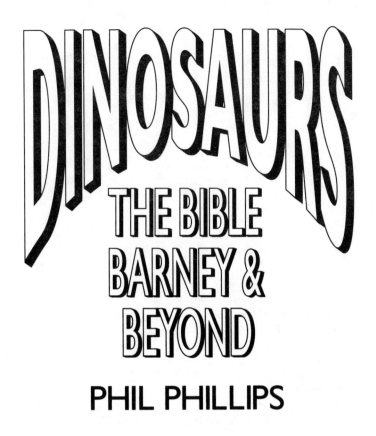

DINOSAURS
THE BIBLE
BARNEY &
BEYOND

PHIL PHILLIPS

STARBURST PUBLISHERS™

P.O. Box 4123, Lancaster, Pennsylvania 17604

To schedule Author appearances write:
Author Appearances, Starburst Promotions, P.O. Box 4123
Lancaster, Pennsylvania 17604 or call (717) 293-0939

Credits:
Cover art by Kerne Erickson

DINOSAURS, THE BIBLE, BARNEY & BEYOND
Copyright ©1994 by Starburst, Inc.
All rights reserved.

First Printing, October 1994

ISBN: 0-914984-59-4
Library of Congress Catalog Number 94-66616
Printed in the United States of America

Dedicated
to
Jane Stoddard . . .

We appreciate your friendship.
Thank you for the part you have played
in our fight for God's children.

Contents

1

Fabulous Creatures From a Fascinating Age

Some were fat, and others thin.
Some were ugly, and others beautiful.
Some were graceful, and others lumbering.
Some were big, others small.

As a whole, they were mysterious, exotic, strange, wild, and frightening. The very idea of them fascinates and excites.

What were they?

Dinosaurs!

And today, they seem to be everywhere!

Dinosaurs have been used to promote just about everything in America, from cereal to gasoline. They have appeared on greeting cards, key chains, and sneakers—virtually anything that can be imprinted, displayed, or worn. Today there's even dinosaur table wear. And products being developed include dinosaur sunglasses, soap, and vitamins.

You and your child are likely to encounter dinosaurs at clothing stores, libraries, doctor's waiting rooms, grocery stores, and national parks, in newspapers and on television, and even on school milk cartons.

Why? Because dinosaurs sell. They sell because they fascinate.

And they particularly seem to intrigue Americans.

The dinosaur craze is not limited to the United States and Canada, but it is focused on these nations. No other nation or continent seems to be as crazed as we are about these creatures from ancient days.

Nobody seems quite sure why we are so interested in dinosaurs and have been for decades. Part of their popularity is perhaps related to the fact that *most* of the dinosaur fossils discovered to date have been found in North America.

Also, American tale spinners have focused more media attention on dinosaurs than their counterparts in other nations, including far more attention on recent extinction theories.

Museums have used dinosaur fossils to spark interest in their other displays.

Movies have been made featuring well-animated replicas of ancient creatures—from the well-known *Jurassic Park* to the 18-foot mechanical pterodactyl, *Quetzalcoatlus northropi* featured in a large-screen movie shown in museum theaters throughout North America.

You may very well find dinosaurs at your local zoo—in the form of a traveling troupe of animated creatures that roar.

Local libraries are sponsoring reading programs that feature dinosaur books.

Dinosaurs are the hot new craze in the world of interior decorating. A line of gilded dinosaurs has been created as drawer pulls, tie backs, and a towel bar!

Even the U.S. Postal Service has participated in the dinosaur rage—issuing a series of four $.25 stamps that featured a *Tyrannosaurus, Stegosaurus, Pteranodon,* and *Brontosaurus.*

No one seems immune to the spell of dinosaurs. And especially so, our children.

While some adults are interested in dinosaurs, and those who are paleontologists have found a way to translate that interest into full-time employment—most dinosaur enthusiasts are children. That's been the case for decades.

Today's children between the ages of 5 and 15 probably know more about the history and behavior of dinosaurs than they do their own grandparents.

Take a peek into a child's room and you may very well find dinosaur posters . . . dinosaur rulers and erasers . . . shelves displaying scale models of the current favorites, *Tyrannosaurus rex, Protoceratops, Triceratops,* and *Velociraptors* . . . T-shirts hanging in the closet with dinosaurs front and back. At snack-time, children are eating dinosaur-shaped cookies.

Again we ask, *why* the fascination?

Certainly one major aspect of the dinosaur appeal is that we simply do not know that much about dinosaurs. Therefore, we can fantasize freely. We know just enough about dinosaurs to be intrigued. And *nobody* can "imagine" quite like a child!

It is precisely because dinosaurs fill the imagination of our children that we adults need to be as fully informed about dinosaurs as we can be.

- We need to know exactly what *is* known about them today . . . and what isn't.
- We need to know the extent of their impact in the media our children encounter.
- And above all, we need to know their place in the philosophies of men and the wisdom of God.

Dinosaurs are with us still.

We need to learn just *how* to live with them in peace.

2

Jurassic Park—
It's One Place You Won't
Want to Take Your Children
for the Afternoon

Jurassic Park, in a nutshell, is the story of a what goes wrong when a wealthy businessman hires a team of scientists to replicate dinosaurs (genetically) and create a theme park.

The movie has been a blockbuster, even by movie giant Steven Spielberg's standards. The real draw of the movie, however, is not the story, but the special effects, and in particular, the masterfully executed dinosaur animation.

The plot of the movie can be summed up in a few words: A former flea-circus operator has developed a high-tech island zoo in which dinosaurs (genetically engineered from blood samples taken from a prehistoric mosquito encased in amber) roam freely. Prior to the official opening of the park, the owner invites three highly respected scientists, the park's attorney, and his own two grandchildren for a premier test-run tour.

Things go amuck when the technology fails and the dinosaurs turn out to be fiercer and much, much smarter than ever anticipated. Meanwhile, one of the computer hackers responsible for engineering the park has turned greedy and seeks to sell dinosaur embryos to a competitor. The hacker meets a bloody end—as do several others—but his betrayal of the project heightens the danger to the staff and guests that remain stranded on the island.

If one strips away the special effects—which are truly spectacular—and the roller-coaster emotions rooted in fear, *Jurassic Park* really doesn't have much of a plot, nor does it offer much in the way of life-impacting characterizations. The movie provides a good scare, but not necessarily a good story.

The viewer never fully understands, for example, just why everybody has to get off the island by the evening ferry. There's no reason given for why so much of the technology has been entrusted to just one person (not at all a realistic situation).

The characters are very thinly drawn and the viewer never really knows:

- the nature of the romantic relationship between the paleontologist and the paleobotanist,
- how it is that the grand-daughter becomes an instantaneous computer whiz (capable of fixing a massive and complex system that is in shambles with just the push of a few command keys),
- why the computer hacker turns greedy and becomes a traitor,
- or why the park owner is willing to accommodate glitches and open the park knowing that not all systems are fully tested (or why he would use his own grandchildren as guinea pigs in the test process).

For that matter, no explanation is really given as to what happens at the movie's opening, other than the fact that someone is obviously hurt badly or killed by an unknown creature.

Based on the Best-Selling Book . . .

The movie is based on a best-selling book by Michael Crichton, *The Making of Jurassic Park*.

The plot, actually, is not unlike that of Crichton's prior works—especially a 1971 film script called *Westworld*. In this movie, robot characters run amuck in a fantasyland resort.

In his first draft of the book, Crichton actually presented the story through the eyes of the children—that is, the entrepreneur character John Hammond's two young grandchildren. The first readers, however, wanted an adult point of view so the book was revised and told from the point of view of the paleontologist character, Alan Grant.

Much more of the book than movie presents the ideas of fictional character Ian Malcolm, an expert in "chaos theory." Crichton admits that the Malcolm character speaks largely with his own voice and mirrors Crichton's belief that "science is in many ways over the top, particularly in its arrogance" (pg. 5, *The Making of Jurassic Park*).

After a fairly intense bidding war for the rights to the book, the picture was "won" by Universal Pictures on behalf of Steven Spielberg. In preparing the script, the book was stripped down to seven or eight scenes. Fifteen dinosaur species were reduced to seven.

Unlike the book—in which the park's setting, "Isla Nublar," is bombed into oblivion—Jurassic Park survives in the movie and the heroes escape. A *Return to Jurassic Park* is left open as a very real possibility.

Violence of the Most Insidious Kind

The foremost characteristic of this movie is its violence. The stalking, "hunting" behavior of the dinosaurs is what makes the movie scary.

That in and of itself may be a feature that adults find appealing. But it is not the characteristic of a movie that is good for children. Furthermore, in viewing *Jurassic Park*, children have been watching other children become truly frightened and in jeopardy of their lives. There's nothing scarier to a child. It's one thing for a child to watch a monster movie or to see adults imperiled. A far more intense reaction is registered when a child watches another child in danger.

Many reviewers of *Jurassic Park* have echoed the sentiment that the movie is too violent for children. The man-chewing, car-crunching scenes are more jarring than *Jaws*, which is certainly not a movie for children.

The "Parent's Guide" review offered by a secular magazine, *Entertainment Weekly*, is worth quoting in its entirety:

"This 'Park' Is No Playground

"The nightmare always starts the same way, Mom. *You're taking me to see Jurassic Park and I look at the front seat and there's Barney the dinosaur. He starts to sing 'I love you, you love me.' But then he starts to sniff me. And his eyes get all funny and his head gets all big. And he says, 'I could just eat you up.' And then he starts biting me and I come apart in his big white teeth . . .*

"Okay, parents, time to feel torn and guilty about a Steven Spielberg movie again. Could *Jurassic Park* possibly give young children some really, really bad dreams? Yes. The movie is rated PG-13, and that seems appropriate, but the ads are going to appeal to kids a lot younger than 13. And this is a really, really scary movie.

"Parents should know, for one thing, that the benevolent, nature-documentary tone of the teaser TV commercials tells only part of the story. Sure, there are several scenes of cute, harmless dinosaurs—but far more of *Jurassic* is devoted to suspense, violence, and heart-pounding frights. If you get on this ride, be prepared for the following nasty jolts:

- A dinosaur pulls a screaming man into its crate to kill him. Carnage is not shown but is strongly suggested.
- A steer is eaten alive by dinosaurs (not shown but heard) and a live goat gets ripped to pieces by a tyrannosaurus (not heard but shown).
- A man is snatched up in a dinosaur's jaws (shown) and eaten alive, to the sound of crunching on the soundtrack.
- A *T. rex* attacks a Ford Explorer tour vehicle with a young boy and girl trapped inside. At various moments, they appear very likely to be crushed, eaten, or suffocated by the muddy ground the dino keeps pushing the car into. The boy is shown bloody from facial injuries and both children appear frightened to the point of shock.
- A severed human limb appears on screen.
- Several dinos jump out at characters for 'gotcha' shock surprises.
- Two children are hunted by two smaller dinosaurs in an extended sequence set in a cafeteria kitchen."—*SD*

(Entertainment Weekly, June 18, 1993, page 22)

Also scary, but not mentioned in this review is a scene in which park owner Hammond's young grandson lets go of a fence just as 10,000 volts course through it. He apparently feels a zap. Experts in electricity say that such a child would be "fried," not just stunned.

And what do the actors and movie makers say about this violence? None of them has stepped forward to either deny or dismiss the impact of the violence. In fact, their nonchalance about the violence has been appalling.

One of the stars in the movie, Sam Neill (who plays paleontologist Alan Grant) is quoted in *Entertainment Weekly* as saying, "The death of the lawyer is one of the funniest things I've ever seen on film. Another is when an arm lands on Laura Dern's shoulder and she thinks to her relief it's Sam Jackson, but, of course, the arm is dismembered. It's absolutely a riot! I'm a sucker for it." (July 23, 1993, page 18)

Not a Children's Movie, And Yet . . .

The foremost fact that seems to be overlooked by just about everybody is this: *Jurassic Park* was never intended for children. The book, which was published in 1991, was not written for children. Its purpose was, to a great extent, to explore the issue of genetic manipulation and the desirability of pursuing research that results in cloning, DNA-replication, and genetic engineering. The author, Michael Crichton, appears throughout the book to have a deep concern about man's apparent desire and attempts to play around with biology. He sees this as a very dangerous enterprise. That's not a children's theme!

The movie was also not created for children—especially young children. Steven Spielberg, the movie's creator, is on record as stating that he has no intent of showing the movie to his own child!

Spielberg has an eight-year-old son. Has he seen the movie? No.

Amy Irving, Spielberg's ex-wife and the mother of their son, Max, said, "I'd never let him see *Jurassic Park*. I went home nauseous after seeing it, it's so scary. It depends on the kid, but Max is a boy who's very sensitive. Max said, 'Daddy said I could see it if I'm in a theater with him and I could walk out.' I asked Steven if this was true and he said, 'Years later! I'm talking about years later! When he's a teenager!'"

One of the most disturbing concerns about *Jurassic Park* is the fact that while the movie was given a PG-13 rating—which suggests that the movie should receive Parental Guidance and has material probably not suited for children under the age of 13—the movie was *marketed* largely as a family film.

All of the teaser information and advertising—including in-theater promotion shown prior to other movies—was scaled back to appeal to a younger audience.

The marketing sweep included a number of firms that deal primarily with *children*—not thirteen-year-olds and older.

Months before the movie was even completed, for example, McDonald's had signed an agreement with the film makers for marketing toys in their "kid meal" packs in support of the movie. McDonald's has spent billions of dollars—in addition to frying billions of hamburgers—in developing a universal reputation as a place that is safe, fun, and wholesome for *children*. To have a child-associated sponsor in support of a teen-rated movie doesn't make sense, and was probably a bad move on the part of the McDonald's. In all probability, McDonald's didn't know fully what was to be the tone or content of the movie. Parents, however, need to be aware that just because a reputable child-oriented firm is linked to a movie, the movie is not necessarily good for children.

Finally, the producers themselves definitely wanted a family-friendly PG-13 rating—even though movie-going research shows that many parents take along children much younger than 13.

To attract this audience, several major changes were made from the book. The book's "early sign of trouble" is the mauling of a Costa Rican baby. In the movie, a Jurassic Park worker is mauled by a caged *Velociraptor*. Still scary, but not as horrific as the mauling of a baby.

In the book, Hammond is nibbled to death by scavenging *Procompsognathids*. Again, movie-makers thought that too horrific and they left Hammond alive to the end.

The scientific explanations are dealt with by an animated character called "Mr. DNA" in the movie, rather than park owner John Hammond, paleontologist Alan Grant, or geneticist Dr. Henry Wu—as in the book. The movie-makers thought the animated figure would be less boring to children.

In my opinion, *Jurassic Park* should have been given an "R" rating. It's root theme is one of terror. Screaming and crying are the usual reactions to the presence of the dinosaurs. The violence factor is R-worthy high—even if much of it lies in the imagination of the viewers.

Big, But It Might Have Been Bigger

There's no doubt that *Jurassic Park* is one of the—if not *the*—biggest hit in movie history. It has the biggest opening weekend—$47 million. It hit $100 million in a record of nine days and $200 million in a record of twenty-three days. It's on a pace to surpass *Star Wars* and *E.T.: The Extra-Terrestrial* in only its first release (compared to their totals that count rereleases). In all, MCA/Universal could gross some $2 billion worldwide, including video revenue and its cut of the retail merchandise.

Jurassic Park represents one of the most complete marketing cycles of any story ever to hit today's media world. The story began as a best-selling hardback book. The movie was released and that spawned a huge paper-back book blitz (with more than seven million copies in print just weeks after the movie's release). Hot on the heels of the story itself was the paperback titled *The Making of Jurassic Park* (a behind-the-scenes look at the movie). Which no doubt will prompt most of its readers to take another look at the movie (or video). All of which lends support for the purchase of spin-off products, games, toys, and children's books.

The movie, as one might expect, had large numbers going into release. It cost about $60 million to make, even without Spielberg taking a salary (prior to opening day and a percentage of the profits) or the use of major stars.

For all of that, not only parents but movie critics agree: *Jurassic Park* could have been bigger. Box office analyst Michael Mahern said it this way in *Entertainment Weekly*, "What if *Jurassic* had the childish wonder of *E.T.*? Old ladies went to see *E.T.* They're not going to *Jurassic Park*" (*Entertainment Weekly*, July 23, 1993, page 16).

For that matter, fairly young children went to see *E.T.*—but *Jurassic Park* definitely isn't targeted toward them or appropriate for them.

And What About The Science?

As stated earlier, the dinosaur recreation (robotic and computer generated) is stunning. In nearly all cases, the dinosaurs truly "look" real. A number of viewers have said to me repeatedly, "The dinosaurs were the best part" and "I only went to see the dinosaurs."

How accurate are the dinosaur depictions?

Surely one of the most interesting discrepancies is that the main dinosaur stars aren't from what scientists call the Jurassic period! They are creatures generally placed in the Cretaceous period.

Scientists generally agree that:

- *Velociraptors* were about six feet in length, half of which was tail. That makes them about the body size of a full-grown German shepherd. The ones in the movie are about twenty feet in total length.

- Dinosaurs weren't smart enough to do what they do in the movie. Even the smartest *Velociraptor* was probably no smarter than an ostrich. And no ostrich has ever opened a door!

And could dinosaurs be cloned as they are in the movie? Scientists seem to agree universally that the premise of the movie is *not* possible.

In Michael Crichton's story, genetic biologists clone dinosaurs from DNA extracted out of blood-sucking insects preserved in amber. If such were possible, a number of dinosaur eggs, with perfectly preserved fetuses of baby dinosaurs inside them, have been discovered through the years—each of which, also, of course, has DNA chains to study.

In the so-called "educational clip" in the movie, Mr. DNA talks about a scientist who drills a hole in a piece of fossilized tree sap and draws out liquid blood. This isn't remotely possible. One scientist, Dr. Ward Wheeler, an assistant curator at the American Museum of Natural History, has spent a lot of time with insects and amber and he has said that the only "liquid" one might withdraw would be liquid first shot *into* the amber in hopes of withdrawing some dried particles with it. He commented, "I've gotten insect DNA that way" but never dinosaur DNA. In fact, the only true link to the scientific research in the movie is that in 1992, two teams of scientists announced that they had, almost simultaneously, recovered bits of DNA from insects encased in amber, which they projected to be thirty million years old.

Still, Spielberg calls the premise behind the movie "science eventuality," rather than science fiction.

Extracting a few genes out of ancient insect DNA strands, however, is a far cry from putting together *dino-*

saur DNA, much less actually unleashing the chain reactions necessary to cause a dinosaur, or any other animal, to come to life. The greater likelihood is that these ancient strands **might** be compared to modern-day species to see how the two relate.

Scientists have cloned a few viruses, bacteria and other individual cells, but they are nowhere close to recreating an organism of more complex design. Even the lowliest of creatures has thousands of genes and to completely copy even a simple organism's genetic blueprint would be an enormous undertaking.

Scientists have also taken an entire DNA-containing nucleus out of a frog cell and inserted it into an egg cell in which the nucleus had been removed. Theoretically, a dinosaur cell with an intact nucleus, might be inserted into the nucleus of a host egg. The assumption, however, is that the dinosaur cell would have to be "alive"—that is, capable of replicating. There's no evidence that this is anywhere near being accomplished.

Rumbling Concerns
Beyond Violence and Faulty Science

Beyond the violence and faulty science, I have four points of very deep concern with this movie:

First, man is depicted as engineering life. While this point is discussed and the conclusion is drawn in a general way that genetics may be an area in which human tampering is inappropriate—the mystery, awe, and wonder of the movie all are on the side of the opinion, "isn't it great that this has been done?" The scientists are enraptured with the process . . . until they are velociraptored!

The conclusion is not, "leave life up to God's plan," but rather, "this attempt went awry, but perhaps man can try again to improve God's design." That's hard-core heresy and not at all unlike the deceit of the serpent in the Garden of Eden.

Second, the movie sends a message, "Nothing ever really dies . . . completely." DNA trapped in blood in a mosquito in a piece of amber . . . is still in some way portrayed as alive. Dinosaurs that are supposedly all of one sex and incapable of reproduction . . . do. The lie of the serpent is simply reinterpreted once again: "You will never die."

Third, the movie presents a number of examples in which man has total disregard for fellow man. The computer-nerd character, Dennis Nedry, is intent upon smuggling out dinosaur DNA for the sake of money, and money alone. Even though he is depicted as a bad guy, the message is never clearly drawn that he is evil—only that he gets caught in his own trap through some fairly clumsy driving on a rainy night. The moral is never explicit that his *motivation* is evil.

The same holds true for the entrepreneur and park owner who "created" Jurassic Park for entertainment purposes. The John Hammond character is never fully depicted as being an evil man—someone intent on taking shortcuts that endanger lives for the sake of profit.

It's difficult *not* to draw a comparison between Hammond, the park developer, and director Spielberg. Hammond is a character who loses sight of his responsibility to his audience in his rise from flea circus operator to the creator of the most innovative and mind-boggling theme park ever built. In many ways, Spielberg seems to have lost sight of his responsibility to movie-going children in his rise to the pinnacle of movie producing.

Fourth, the movie reinforces a number of stereotypes that aren't particularly accurate or wholesome. The nervous, selfish attorney—a character called Donald Gennaro—

is a stereotyped lawyer of the 1990's. The movie-going audience has little sympathy for him and his bloody demise. The computer hacker is a sloppy, gluttonous obese person—again, a character frequently stereotyped in our culture as "bad." In reality, obese people are just as capable of being good as being evil, and not all lawyers are selfish.

And What About Chaos Theory?

One of the most accurate aspects of the movie is the rather "boring" fact that there really is a chaos theory. James Gleick popularized the subject in a 1987 best-seller titled *Chaos: Making a New Science*. In a nutshell, the theory proposes that even the tiniest changes in nature can have vast consequences. For example, the flapping of a butterfly's wings in New York City might help effect a weather change halfway around the globe over the course of a month.

Those who believe in God's continued control of the universe wouldn't regard this as chaos, however, but divine *order*. Every action impacts every other action. The Bible is a book that emphasizes the word "we." God's people are a collective. His universe has a rhythm and order to it that operates as a whole. There is nothing about *Jurassic Park*, however, that factors in God. From cloning to chaos to car-crunching to Cretaceous creeps . . . there's no mention of Creator. God is rather conspicuously barred from this park.

3

Elsewhere on the Big Screen: Dinosaurs Lumber On and Destroy

Jurassic Park is by no means the first major dinosaur movie to have mass public appeal. The history of movie making has been dotted with dinosaurs in modern-day environments. *Gorgo* was the story of a mama dinosaur coming after her baby who had been captured for use in a circus. *Godzilla*, of course, is perhaps the best known of the old dinosaur movies—very realistic in its impact.

One of the things that perhaps makes *Jurassic Park* so scary—and especially to young children—is the fact that it is *not* a "monster movie." From the outset, the designers sought, in the words of production designer Rick Carter, to "find the animal in the dinosaur as opposed to the monster in the dinosaur. The idea was not to make them any less threatening, but rather to keep them from doing as much monster 'schtick.' For our human characters, we wanted their situation to be more like they were being stalked by an animal that is a carnivore, as opposed to something that is psychopathic and just out to get them" (pg. 14, *The Making of Jurassic Park*).

It's to this very end that character Alan Grant explains to the children in the movie, "They're not monsters. They're just animals."

The fact is, the natural world is far more violent than most of us want to think about—and far more violent than most children know or can imagine. There's nothing funny or "fake" about the monsters on Spielberg's screen, and while that may make for superb film-making and special-effects kudos from adults, it also is the basis for a great deal more **fear** on the part of children.

The more realistic the portrayal, the scarier a movie is. The most frightening footage of all tends to be that which is done in National Geographic style—with one species ripping apart another species, spewing blood and guts in all directions. True . . . but not necessarily edifying for young children, and certainly not the kind of thing that makes for a peaceful night's sleep for the average five-year old!

An Emphasis on Certain Traits = Artistic License

Anyone who has seen *Jurassic Park* is sure to recognize the immense artistry in the creation of the dinosaurs—their physical appearance, their animation (from robotics to computer generation), and the editing together of media that makes the dinosaur creatures not only appear lifelike, but with personality.

The *Brachiosaur* that awakens Grant and the two children in a tree is a gentle beast, especially when compared to the *Velociraptors*. In the words of their creator, puppet master Stan Winston, "One is a piranha, the other is a cow." He says of other dinosaurs, "The *Triceratops* is a much gentler character—someone you care about—than a 9,000-pound *Tyrannosaurus rex* who could swallow you in a bite. Their performance, their body language, how they do what they do, determines their character.

It's easy to assume that because the creatures are so detailed that they are firmly rooted in scientific fact, and that these creatures acted, looked, and sounded exactly as they now appear in the movie version. That's far from the case. The truth is that we simply **do not know** what any dinosaur sounded like. We also do not know how they moved—precisely—or with what kind of speed. We aren't one hundred percent sure which ones (if any) were aggressive hunters, and which ate meat as scavengers. We certainly don't know how a *T-rex* responded to light or motion. The ability of a *Velociraptor* to open a laboratory door is a great artistic leap!

Long Tradition of Error in Dinosaur Movies

Unfortunately movie viewers have been desensitized to the scientific error that has permeated the big screen for several generations. It's as the old saying goes, "Tell a lie long enough and often enough and it begins to sound like truth."

Dinosaur movies were among the first movies made. *Gertie the Dinosaur* and *The Dinosaur and the Missing Link* were silent short subjects made nearly ninety years ago.

The first of the great dinosaur films was *The Lost World*, released in 1925 after seven years in production. The story mirrored the Sir Arthur Conan Doyle 1912 novel by the same name: an English expedition led by a hot-tempered scientist and explorer named Professor Challenger, locates a South American plateau inhabited by prehistoric monsters. The expedition manages to capture a *Brontosaurus* and barely escaping the plateau with their lives, they return to London with the creature, where it breaks loose and creates panic in the streets. The movie was a sensation in its day and racked in big box-office receipts. It was a marvel of what was called "stop-motion," the animation process pioneered by the French film maker Georges Melies and perfected by Willis H. O'Brien. The movie would appear crude by today's standards, but it was a remarkable visual feat in its day. Approximately fifty "monsters" were created for the movie.

The film that really sparked renewed interest in "fantasy creatures" was *King Kong*, the landmark movie of the 1930's. The story is amazingly close to that of *The Lost World*. This time the expedition is to the uncharted ocean west of Sumatra, where the group lands on Skull Island. The beast is transported back to New York instead of London.

The description of Kong is typical of the verbage often used to describe dinosaurs: "Neither beast nor man . . . something monstrous, all-powerful . . . still living, still holding that island in the grip of deadly fear."

Kong battles a *Tyrannosaurus,* a *Pteranodon*, and an anonymous snakelike cave creature . . . and wins. A *Stegosaurus* charges the expedition, and a *Brontosaurus* pulls screaming men into a swamp (becoming a carnivore rather than the herbivore known to science).

In the 1940's, the best dinosaur "movie" was probably one of the segments in *Fantasia*, Walt Disney's animated sequence set to classical music. In the segment depicting the dawn of creation, Igor Stravinsky's 1912 *Rite of Spring* plays under a battle between a *Stegosaurus* and a *Tyrannosaurus rex*. The New York Academy of Science asked for a copy of the segment to use because they thought the dinosaurs were "better science" than a whole museum of fossils and taxidermy!

Dinosaur movies proliferated in the 1950s, including a rerelease of *King Kong* (its fourth release and one that was highly lucrative) and *Journey to the Center of the Earth* (1959). Stock footage was made available from *One Million*

B.C.—the dinosaur scenes from which were recycled numerous times!

The 1960's was an era of dinosaur spoofs, such as *Dinosaurus!* In the 1970s, very few dinosaur films were issued. Most notable were probably *When Dinosaurs Ruled the Earth* (1970) which won an Oscar nomination for effects, and *The Land that Time Forgot* (1975), based on an Edgar Rice Burroughs 1918 novel. In the 1980s, *The Land Before Time* (1988) was probably the best-known dinosaur movie, even though it was animated and for children.

What needs to be said about these old movies is this: Most of the dinosaur behavior and appearance depicted in them is outdated scientifically.

Other Recent Big-Screen Dinosaur Flicks

Steven Spielberg and Amblimation, a subsidiary of his Amblin Entertainment, released yet another Spielberg dinosaur film in 1993—this time an animated feature about a time-traveling group of dinosaurs titled *We're Back! A Dinosaur's Story.*

My great fear is that parents who admit that *Jurassic Park* was too violent for young children will think that this movie is alright for little ones simply because it is an animated feature with a G rating. *We're Back!* is definately not a good one for children, as far as I am concerned.

The movie, now available on video, is the story of a futuristic professor named New Eyes who feeds a cereal-like substance called brain grain to four dinosaurs: Rex *(a T-rex)*, Elsa *(a pterydactyl)*, Dweeb*(a platypus)*, and Woog *(a triceratops)*. While listening to the professor's Wish Radio, the now-brilliant dinosaurs hear children in the Middle Future—our present age—wishing they could see dinosaurs. They agree to time travel to earth to appear in a special scientific exhibition so that these children can have their wishes come true.

On earth, they make friends with Louie and Cecelia, two lonely and wayward children who are intent upon running away from home to join the Van Demon Circus, which is run by Processor New Eyes' evil brother, Professor Screw Eyes. Called the master of fear, Professor Screw Eyes has a Fright Radio and feeds "brain drain" to children. The brain drain is packaged in pills, similar to some illegal drugs. It has the capacity to capture ideas and take control of a person's willpower. In taking brain drain, Louie and Cecelia turn into monkeys.

The four dinosaurs, feeling compassion for their friends, agree to take brain drain and become captives of the evil professor if the children are returned to normal.

The children give "healing hugs" to the dinosaurs and in Cecelia's wishing, "Let no bad happen," Professor New Eyes is brought to earth and to the rescue. Crows completely cover Professor Screw Eyes and seemingly devour him. When they fly away, he has disappeared, except for his false eye, which bounces across the ground.

The theme music that plays over the credits is titled "Roll Back and Rock," a song with a straight-evolution storyline sung by old-time rock singer Little Richard.

The premise of this movie *appears* to be good—a message that running away and joining up with those who give you "brain drain"substances results in no good. I have several major concerns, however. The movie depicts occultic symbols and language, promotes evolution, and offers a very cheap solution to drug addiction of drug experimentation: wishes and hugs. The implication is that it is just as easy for a person to get out of a drug-induced stupor as it is to get into one. That simply is not the case.

There's yet another highly disturbing message: it's acceptable to do something that you know is harmful to your body as long as your motive is to help others. This is the old ends-aren't-related-to-means moral justification argument. When it comes to drugs, a child should be given a message that it is never good to take mind-altering chemicals, regardless of motive.

Of somewhat less concern spiritually but still of concern is the message that a substance such as brain grain can make a person smart. This substance in the movie looks very much like today's cereal products, which tend to be laden with sugar and are anything but good for a child's mental capacities!

Unfortunately, some very well-known personalities have lent their voices to this movie, including Walter Cronkite, Julia Child, John Goodman, Martin Short, Jay Leno, and Rhea Perlman.

Also from the recent big screen and now available in video is a horror flick titled *Carnosaur.* This is a tale about a dinosaur-obsessed mad geneticist, played by Diane Ladd, who creates a T-rex in her genetics lab. They multiply like rats in a small town, creating a war-to-the-death environment. This movie is bloody and R-rated, yet the video box illustration appeals to children and teens. Don't be fooled.

Dino Movies in the Future

What can we expect in the wake of the *Jurassic Park*-inspired resurgence of interest in dinosaur-related movies?

There is little on the immediate horizon to suggest that any of the past factual errors about dinosaurs are about to be remedied.

Spielberg is the executive producer of the movie version—live action, this time, rather than animation—of *The*

Flinstones. The movie is based on the television series of the 1960's and stars John Goodman as Fred Flinstone, Rick Moranis as his side-kick friend Barney, Elizabeth Perkins as Wilma Flinstone, Elizabeth Taylor as Wilma's mom, and Rosie O'Donnel as Betty Rubble. The dinosaurs are being designed by the same computer artist group that did *Jurassic Park*: Industrial Light & Magic, along with the Henson Group Creature Shop.

Godzilla is being redone by TriStar Pictures. Of course, Godzilla is technically a monster rather than a dinosaur, but the similarities are remarkable.

T. Rex is a film about a New York City police woman who has a mild-mannered *Tyrannosaurus* as her partner. They uncover a plot to destroy the world.

The fact is, as with all movies, movies about dinosaurs are made to emphasize certain of their characters and to present the traits of these creatures that the *movie maker* finds the most interesting (or believes will be most interesting to the viewer).

Areas in which facts are unknown are "filled in with speculation, guesswork, and imagination."

What Should Warrant Our Concern?

Movies are stories, not documentaries. We need to be aware that **most** of what we see on the screen, and especially what we see about dinosaurs, is not likely to be rooted in reality.

That's a message adults readily understand, of course, but it is **not** the way children watch movies. Children believe in the fantastic. They frequently are incapable of separating fact from fiction. In watching movies with our children—and especially movies about dinosaurs—we need to continually pull our children in for a "reality check."

We need to have heightened concern when imagination is channeled into messages that evoke:

- fear,
- a tolerance of violence (and especially depictions of violence rooted in rebellion),
- a twisted view of God's creation, or
- a fantasy that opens up a person to the power of the occult, and to evil.

These messages are the ones that need to send chills running up and down our spines. These are the messages we need to shield our children against!

There are those who believe that dinosaurs are *God's* monsters—that they were biological marvels and supernatural beasts intended to evoke fear and awe.

The approach that the Bible takes consistently, however, is that God did not design any creature to instill "fear" in mankind. Man was always to have dominion over the animal kingdom—something that simply would not have been possible in the prehistoric world most artists and scientists depict.

The Bible speaks equally clear about the origin of deep-seated fear: the enemy of our souls, Satan himself. He is the one described as a stalking "roaring lion, seeking whom he may devour"—a predatory, scary creature intent upon our destruction and death. (See John 10:10 and I Peter 5:8.)

The Bible's teachings about violence and rebellion are clear. Neither is to have root in us. Likewise, we are to run from evil, and refuse to open ourselves up "even a bit" to that which gives power or influence to our Enemy.

Unfortunately, most of what is shown of dinosaurs on the big screen *is* intended to evoke fear. Dinosaurs are nearly always portrayed as violent and evil.

A simple rule of thumb can be applied here: Until you've screened a dinosaur movie yourself, don't let your child experience it.

4

Fossils and Those Who Study Them: What Do We Really Know for Sure?

Perhaps the foremost fact we know about dinosaurs is also the simplest fact: they *did* exist. We have their remains.

Everything we think we know about dinosaurs comes from bones—most of which are fossilized—and fossilized footprints. In some cases, these bones and prints were once buried deep in the earth. But given time, erosion, and shifts in the earth's plates, they are now much closer to the earth's surface. In other cases, man hadn't found the fossils because he wasn't looking for them. The fossils tell us, in very direct and simple terms: dinosaurs once roamed most *all* regions of the earth.

What has actually been found in the fossil beds?

> Bones
> Bony plates
> Claws
> Dung (coprolite)
> Eggs
> Feather imprints (very rare)
> Footprints
> Gastroliths (stones that acted like "gizzards" in digestion)
> Horns

Plant and tree (imprints)
Skin imprints (very rare)
Spikes
Stomach contents (very rare)
Teeth
Unborn young

In some cases, bone marrow has been fossilized with the bones. Tree fossils, of course, include some bark imprints.

What do these rock bones and footprints tell us?

Some Dinosaurs Were Massive

One of the main facts revealed by dinosaur fossils is no doubt the fact that fascinates us the most: some dinosaurs were huge. In fact, they were downright massive. Nothing on earth today rivals them for size. To think that creatures of this magnitude once roamed the earth freely is, indeed, a frightening and intriguing thought.

Consider these statistics:

- The *Ultrasaurus* was so big that a giraffe could walk between its legs without ducking. It was as long as three school buses, weighed more than twenty elephants, and had a nine-foot-long shoulder blade.

- A *T-rex* incisor has been found that was eleven inches long. Imagine a mouth with sixty such teeth in a three-foot-wide jaw.

- An *Hypselosaurus* egg has been found that is twelve inches long and could have made an omelet that would serve thirty-six people!

- The neck of *Mamenchisaurus* was longer than a tennis court is wide.

- The *Diplodocus* had a forty-five-foot-long tail, nearly the length of five compact cars.

- *Stegosaurus* was thirty feet long and weighed two ton (4,000 pounds). His brain, however, was only the size of a walnut.
- *Deinocherus* literally means "terrible hands." This creature had 9-foot-long arms and 12-inch-long claws. Scientists believe it was bigger than the *Tyrannosaurus.*
- The *Quetzalcoatlus* had a wing span of forty feet.
- The club on the end of *Euplocephalus' tail was as big as a bicycle.*
- *Triceratops* had eyes as big as baseballs.

King of the dinosaurs in *size,* were the *sauropods,* a family of dinosaurs that included the *Barapausaurus* (which weighed as much as three elephants and had a neck that was so long it could reach the tops of trees twenty feet tall). The bones of this dinosaur were first found in India.

The largest of the *sauropods* is the *Brachiosaurus.* It stood more than forty feet tall and weighed about forty-five tons—that's equal to about twenty mini-vans piled up together. (The bones of an especially large *Brachiosaurus* were found in Colorado, and it was named "Ultrasaurus.")

A large first-cousin named *Seismosaurus,* which literally means "earth-shaking lizard," was found in New Mexico. *Mamenchisaurus,* the bones of which were found in China, has the longest dinosaur neck discovered—a neck almost as long as the rest of its body plus tail.

Dinosaurs Had Unusual Physical Features

Dinosaur fossils have also revealed that these creatures had interesting and unusual physical features.

Some dinosaurs seemed covered with knobs and plates of bone, and occasionally sharp spikes. These are the creatures of the *Ankylosaur* family. One member of the family called *Edmontonia* was probably about as heavy as a pick-up truck, but had very dainty little scalloped teeth in square jaws. Scientists assume it ate a lot of berries or nipped off tough leaves and ate them whole. This creature apparently also ate stones, which may have helped it digest food. (Polished stones were found with one skeleton.)

The *Hadosaurs* or "duck bills" had long flat snouts that made their heads look a little like those of ducks. Unlike ducks, however, they had lots of teeth—as many as two thousand arranged in many rows. Plant-eaters, they probably ate twigs and tough land plants—even pine needles and berry bushes. What scientists don't know is exactly how each duckbill's head may have been adorned. Each of the thirty species had a different head shape. Some appear to have had tall hollow crests atop their heads. These may have been brightly colored.

Replicas of some of the crests have been made and blown into—the result, a variety of sounds similar to trumpets and trombones. Duckbill herds may have been quite noisy!

The *Struthiomimus* are called "ostrich" dinosaurs because they were built much the way ostriches are today. They had sharp beaks but no teeth, and long legs, necks, and arms—which probably made them quite speedy. Since the *Struthiomimus* have no teeth, scientists aren't at all sure what they ate—perhaps small birds, perhaps insects, perhaps even the eggs of other creatures.

Among the fossils found in Wyoming are those in a sedimentary layer known as the "Redwater Shale Member of the Sundance Formation" near the present-day town of Lookout. The sea monster called *Baptanodon— the fastest, most advanced of the ichthyosaurs* or "fish lizards"—was discovered there. This was a seagoing reptile with a large porpoise-shaped body and long narrow snout that hunted at dusk. Its eyeballs were as big across as dinner plates and it apparently swam in a pod of five or ten such creatures.

Noncompeting species in the Sundance Sea were the *Plesiosaur*, or "swan lizards," creatures with much smaller mouths and a much bigger size (weighing up to five tons). *Pliosaur* had a two-foot head, a fifteen-foot neck, and a seven-foot body, with an ugly snout, a buck-toothed display of teeth, and flippers that made the creature seem to fly through the water.

Some Were Huge, But Most Were Small

The large dinosaurs fascinate us most. But the fact is, fossils indicate that *most* dinosaurs were small.

The *Saltopus* was probably no bigger than a large housecat. The vast majority of dinosaurs, at least as far as the fossil record shows thus far, were probably less than fifteen feet long (not including their tails). Many people never even see the fossils of small dinosaurs in museums because they are so intent on looking at the huge skeletons on display.

A Possible Understanding of Dinosaur Skin

Canadian paleontologists found dinosaur skin imprints in the soft rock of Alberta and from this information, a twenty six-foot-tall *Albertasaurus* was squeezed into existence, drop by drop, from a hand-held syringe in an effort to duplicate the texture of her skin. The creature is on exhibit in the Royal Tyrrell Museum in Canada.

The skin impressions have yielded no evidence of hair or feathers—rather, only impressions that their skin was boringly scaly. Some scientists believe, however, that a number of dinosaurs we regard as reptiles may have been birds, given the comparison of their skeletons to those of modern-day birds.

Hints at Dinosaur Behavior and Speed

What else do we know? We know a *little* about their behavior.

Means of Reproduction. We know that dinosaurs laid eggs, since a number of fossilized eggs, and even entire nests, have been found.

As reptiles, dinosaurs were born very small. We have no idea how many eggs were laid at a time, or how frequently, but we do know this about eggs: the larger the egg, the thicker the shell has to be, and the harder, therefore, it is for the hatchling to break out of an egg. Eggs from medium-sized dinosaurs appear to have been about the size of a turkey egg. The largest egg found of the thirty-nine-foot *Hypselosaurus* was only twelve inches long.

Dinosaur eggs, by the way, are very much in vogue these days. A recent auction of them yielded thousands of dollars for large eggs or "nests." Perhaps the greatest find of dinosaur nests was in Devil's Coulee, about 190 miles south of Calgary, Canada, where more than a dozen dinosaur nests yielded up to twenty cantaloupe-sized eggs each. The eggs were those of duckbill dinosaurs, a herbivore that grew to thirty-three feet.

Community Behavior. Researchers believe that many of the dinosaur species traveled in herds and were highly protective of their young. Remains of one mother *Hadrosaur* were found frozen in time atop eggs she apparently tried to protect from a landslide.

Four *Deinonychus* remains were found with their assumed prey, a large plant-eating creature, suggesting that these sharp-clawed carnivores hunted or scavenged in groups.

Maiasaura bone beds reveal that these dinosaurs probably roamed in gigantic herds.

Intelligence. Some dinosaurs may have been more intelligent than our modern-day horse, but most appear to have been fairly dim-witted.

Troodon fossils reveal a human-sized carnivore that boasted a brain case larger than any animal known to be alive in that era, making it perhaps the most intelligent of dinosaurs.

Most dinosaurs had small brains in comparison to the size of their bodies. For example, the twenty-nine-foot *Stegosaurus* had a brain the size of a walnut. Even the huge *sauropods*, such as *Brachiosaurus*, had brains the size of a kitten. This does not necessarily mean that these animals were stupid. But, their function was probably highly specialized, and they certainly were not capable of *outwitting* a human being.

Scientists, of course, draw conclusions about brain function from brain size, and they deduce brain size based upon the size of cranial cavities found in skull bones.

Speed. Tracks have been measured—with fairly elaborate formulas—to conclude that some dinosaurs may have moved as fast as forty miles per hour (similar to a horse galloping at top speed).

Bones Can Tell About Motion

Fossils reveal in a number of ways how a creature may have been able to move.

- Scientists are able to determine from neck bones if the creature could pivot its head.
- Strong shoulder bones and heavy front legs indicate an ability to charge, and thrust with power.
- Large leg bones means that a dinosaur can move on land, and usually run for extended periods of time.

- Creatures with big shoulder bones and points of attachment for large shoulder muscles are considered to be capable of holding a tight grip.
- Long hind legs (especially linked to short front legs) can indicate an ability to jump, pounce, kick, or run quickly.
- Claws, of course, and specifically their position, reveal how the animal may have either stripped bark or flesh.

A mixture of bone sizes at a sight is used as an indication that the young stayed with their parents for a long period of time. Clusters of bones indicate herding. The shape and wear of teeth indicates what creatures may have eaten. Fossilized tracks indicate in what patterns an animal may have moved.

And finally, the spread of the rib cage gives a clue to the capacity of the lungs and the related heart size.

Meat or Plants for Lunch? Teeth Talk

Much about dinosaur behavior is conjecture based on the type of teeth dinosaurs had. For example, the *Lesothosaurus* had smooth, pointed front teeth, the kind needed to nip off green leaves. The teeth along the sides of the jaws were shaped more like arrowheads, useful for munching and slicing up leaves once in the mouth. Some *Lesothosaurus* fossilized teeth are worn down and scratched. Others are smoother and look unused. Thus, scientists deduce that *Lesothosaurus* probably lost its worn out teeth and grew new ones. In order for that to happen and the dinosaur to remain alive, it probably hibernated.

Heterodontosaurus had three kinds of teeth: sharp front teeth for nipping leaves, ridged back teeth for crunching and mashing, and in between, fangs. Fangs are normally associated with meat eaters, and yet everything about the *Heterodontosaurus* remains indicate a plant-eater.

Scientists then conclude that the *Heterodontosaurus* may have used its fangs for fighting when attacked.

Large rough places on bones show where strong muscles were attached and the shape of jaw bones tell how a dinosaur chewed, and thus, what it probably ate.

Another difference between meat-eaters and plant-eaters is the size of the stomach, determined by bone sizes that encased the abdomen. Meat-eaters have small stomachs, since meat digests quickly—plant-eaters large ones.

Plant-eating dinosaurs tended to have rows of tiny teeth, one species had up to 2,000 teeth (a jaw that looks a lot like a bread knife).

Droppings also give clues. Plant-eating dinosaurs tend to leave behind big, mushy mounds of droppings. Meat-eating dinosaurs left behind coil-shaped droppings.

Dinosaur Names Give Clues to Characteristics

Much that is known about a species is usually reflected in the "name" given to the fossil creature, at least at the time of its discovery.

The original word for "dino" was "deinos"—which means "fearfully great" and then was later interpreted as meaning "terrible." The word "saurus" means "lizard." Taken together, the word "dinosaur" means "terrible lizard." That was the original understanding of dinosaurs.

Although we use the word dinosaurs to refer to all ancient creatures now extinct, *Dinosauria* is actually a very specific group of reptiles. Strictly speaking, the flying *Pterosaurs* and acquatic *Plesiosaurs* are not dinosaurs. Neither are *Mosasaurs, Icthyosaurs,* or *Pelycosaurs.*

Dinosaurs were land-based vertebrates.

Most of the dinosaur names are taken directly from their scientific "genus" names—a genus being a group of organisms that have numerous common characteristics and which are generally regarded as being so much alike that they can breed.

The genus *Allosaurus*, for example, might have specific species *Allosaurux atrox, Allosaurus fragilis, and perhaps even Allosaurusamplexus*—creatures that may have looked and behaved differently, but which are alike in the same way that the *Panthera tigris* and *Panthera leo*—what we know as the tiger and lion—are alike.

Here are three dinosaur names and what they mean:

- *Massopondylus* means "massive vertebra."
- *Tyrannosaurus rex* literally means "tyrant lizard king." Tyrant is "tyranno." Lizard is "saurus." And king is "rex."
- *Lagosuchus* means "rabbit crocodile."

Other dinosaurs have the names of the **place** in which they were found or the **name** of the person who made the find as part of their name.

A Study Only 175 Years Old

Dinosaurs may have lived long ago, but the study of them is very "young."

Paleontologists—scientists who study ancient fossilized animals—have been studying dinosaur remains for only about 175 years. Their science is not an **exact** science and that's an important point to recognize. Paleontologists have no live samples to study. Everything they conjecture about dinosaurs, therefore, must be **inferred**.

This is not to say that people prior to the 1800's did not occasionally come across fossilized remains. In ancient China, vertebrate remains were identified as "dragon bones" and believed to have medicinal powers. In 1676, the Reverend Robert Plot published what now appears to be the upper hind leg bone of a *Megalosaurus*, which he incorrectly assumed was part of a giant human being that once lived on the earth.

In 1787 a publication reported the discovery of a large thigh bone in New Jersey, but unfortunately, the bone disappeared.

In 1770, in a quarry in the Netherlands, a Doctor Hoffman found a jawbone that was not only massive, but unidentifiable. In 1795, the artifact was removed by occupying French forces and taken to Paris, where it was later studied in the early 1800's by Baron Georges Cuvier, a comparative anatomy professor. He identified the fossil as a "mastadon" bone and used the artifact as the cornerstone of his theory of "extinction." Prior to that time, the concept of species extinction had not been defined, as far as we know.

Cuvier, by the way, is considered the first paleontologist, and the founder of paleontology.

Mantell's "Iguanodon"

The first known dinosaur fossil bones were found by Dr. Mantell and his wife Mary Anne. Dr. Mantell was a medical doctor, but he and his wife enjoyed collecting fossils. One day in 1822, they found a rock with a fossil tooth in it. They dug further in the area where they found the tooth and eventually had a collection of teeth and a few bones . . . but no idea as to what kind of creature they had unearthed.

They went to visit Cuvier in Paris, who concluded the fossils were from animals buried suddenly during a terrible flood. He also noted that the fossils were strange, unlike any animal he had studied. He concluded that the fossil bones might have belonged to an extinct variety of hippopotamus and the teeth an extinct variety of rhinoceros.

Three years later, Dr. Mantell met a man who studied lizards in Mexico and Central America, and he showed him his collection of teeth. This man thought the teeth looked like iguana teeth, only much larger. Dr. Mantell named his creature "fossil iguana" or *Iguanodon*.

When Baron Cuvier heard of this, he admitted his original determination may not have been right, and he predicted that a whole new group of fossil animals would be discovered.

Buckland's "Megalosaurus"

A short while later, one of England's most respected scientists, William Buckland, received a large fossilized lower jaw which had been excavated from a mine in the small Oxford village of Stonesfield. Buckland, a professor at Oxford University, noted that it was obviously reptil-ian—the recurved teeth set in sockets were like the teeth of crocodiles and were obviously replaced throughout life in the reptilian manner. He named the fossil *Magalosaurus* ("giant lizard") in 1824.

It is interesting to note that Buckland was a Christian who believed the Bible and wrote a number of books show-ing the evidence of God's design in minerals and rocks.

Owens Comes Up With a Name

As further bones began to surface and be studied, Pro-fessor Richard Owen began to put together what he re-garded as a new class of animals. Owen concluded that although the creatures were reptilian-like, their legs were not held out at the side of the body in a typical reptilian sprawling pose. Rather, they were tucked neatly under-neath the creature's body, mammalian style. Thus, these "giant lizards" did not drag their bodies along the ground, but walked clear of the ground on vertical legs. Thus, they formed their own classification of creatures.

Some twenty years after the Mantells' discovery, Sir Richard Owen suggested a name for all fossil reptiles: *Dinosauria.*

The Great Dinosaur Bone Rush "Out West"

Dinosaurs became a major scientific pursuit in the late 1800s.

Much of fossil research developed from an intense rivalry between two East-coast scientists: Edward Cope and Othniel Charles Marsh. Cope, working out of Philadelphia, eventually contracted for bones that led him to the identification of fifty-six new species (and the study of more than a thousand species). Marsh, working at Yale, identified eighty new species from the bones that he obtained. Where did the men get their fossils? First, from quarry and mine workers in the Pennsylvania and New Jersey areas, and later from prospectors in the Northwest. Both men, by the way, were avid evolutionists.

It wasn't until 1887 that a *complete* dinosaur skeleton was uncovered.

One of the richest fossil beds was found by Earl Douglas in Utah. He shipped some 350 tons of bones from his excavation to the Carnegie Museum.

The man who has found more dinosaur fossils than anyone else in history, however, is a man who is still very much alive—Jack Horner. It was in 1982 that Horner (in his thirties at the time) discovered a bone bed containing more than 10,900 duckbill dinosaur fossils.

Maiasaura, which literally means "good mother lizard"—is the name Horner gave to a new species of duckbilled dinosaur. He discovered that the ends of some of the young hatchlings' leg bones had not yet finished forming at the time of their demise, indicating that they were unable to walk. Broken bits of eggshell in the nest suggested that the clutch stayed in the nest long after they hatched. The nests Horner found were spaced about twenty feet apart, the average length of an adult *Maiasaura*, suggesting that the dinosaurs nested in a tightly knit rookery like modern penguins. Horner even found a mass that he conjectures may be fossilized food a mother dinosaur was attempting to feed her young.

The bones of the duckbills were found in a fine mud made of volcanic ash, which indicated to the paleontologists that the creatures were caught by an erupting volcano and perished *en masse*.

Where Have Most of the Fossils Been Found?

Montana, and the areas stretching to its north and south, seem especially rich in dinosaur fossils.

Geologists tell us that in the ancient past, much of Kansas was under water—which is why that state has yielded a number of *Pterodactyl* fossils. (The *Pterodactyl* were seafaring, high flying winged creatures.) To the west of Kansas was a huge coastal plain edged between the inland sea and the Rocky Mountains. Along that strip of land roamed the great dinosaurs that are so popular today. In fact, all of the *Tyrannosaurus rex* fossils ever unearthed have been found in that stretch of land. Also unearthed have been the world's largest *sauropods*, including the long-tailed *Apatosaurus (Brontosaurus)* and the *Triceratops, Stegosaurus,* and many others.

Although dinosaur remains have been found from Antarctica to the Arctic Circle, and from the Gobi Desert to New Jersey, that strip of western interior is considered to be the richest source of dinosaur fossils in the world. The work of ancient glaciers and subsequent erosion by wind and water, created the conditions that have resulted in the amazing discoveries of the past century.

Museums are the Real "Jurassic Park" of Today

The real Jurassic Park is probably in Canada—although a strong case can be made for the Utah-Colorado border.

Between 1910 to 1917 some thirty-five new species of "terrible lizards" were discovered in a desolate region thirty miles northeast of Brooks, Canada. This area is now called Dinosaur Provincial Park. It is one of the richest fossil bone beds in the world. One of virtually every dinosaur family known was entombed there and more than 300 complete specimens were unearthed.

It's difficult to imagine, but in times past, large numbers of dinosaurs apparently thrived beside the balmy shore of a shallow tropical inland sea in the heart of what is now called Canada's "bad lands."

Dinosaur Provincial Park is not only a paleontologist's dream, but a 16,000-acre park where visitors can watch important dinosaur finds being prepared in the Field Station, along with dynamic displays that depict what life was once like in the area. The park is two hours southeast of Drumheller.

In the United States, Dinosaur National Monument—a 325-square mile national park on the Utah-Colorado border, is perhaps the best place to view remains of dinosaurs. The Dinosaur's Quarry Visitor Center has remains of *Stegosaurus* skeletons, as well as *Apatosaurus* (commonly called *Brontosaurus*) and *Allosaurus* (a smaller cousin of *Tyrannosaurus rex*) still embedded in the rocks. Visitors are able to watch paleontologists uncovering new specimens daily.

Another place to scout out dinosaurs is Glen Rose, a small community just swventy-five miles southwest of Dallas. In "Dinosaur Valley," paleontologists come from around the world to study dinosaur tracks left in the river bottom. Other places have more or bigger tracks, but the ones in Dinosaur Valley are extremely clear. The tracks reveal the dinosaur's herd instincts, with the larger animals walking on the outside of a herd. Glen Rose officials are quick to point out that more can be learned about the *behavior* of dinosaurs from their fossilized tracks than from their bones.

Museums are big into dinosaurs these days.

Canada's Royal Tyrrell Museum has the largest display of dinosaur specimens in the world. Many of the fossils on display were found in Alberta province. The museum has a very rare complete skeleton of Tyrannosaurus rex. Colorful murals show what the dinosaurs might have looked like on ancient earth, and the museum has fifteen mini-theaters and twenty electronic games.

Calgary has a section of its zoo called "Prehistoric Park," where twenty-six life-size models of extinct creatures seem to meander among the meadows.

The American Museum of Natural History, just off Central Park in New York City, has just remodeled its dinosaur displays and has assembled the world's tallest dinosaur exhibit—a fifty-foot-high, plant-eating *Barosaurus* rearing up on its hind legs to protect its baby from an attacking, meat-eating *Allosaurus*. The *Barosaurus* was discovered in Utah in the 1920's, eighty percent intact, and it is the most complete example of that particular species in the world.

Field Museum of Natural History in Chicago has the world's largest mounted dinosaur: a giraffe-like *Brachiosaurus* that measures seventy-five feet long and forty feet high. It weights eighty-five tons. The remains were discovered in Grand Junction, Colorado.

The Audubon Institute in New Orleans has an exhibit of animated, outdoor robotic dinosaurs that move with the aid of pistons, air tubes, and electrical wiring. The displays include an *Allosaurus* (which literally means "leaping lizard"), an *Apatosaurus* ("deceptive lizard"), a *Deinonychus* (about human size), a *Pteranodon* (one of the largest flying creatures that ever lived with a wing span of thirty feet), a *Stegosaurus* (which used spikes in its tail for self-defense), a *Triceratops* (a three-horned creature with one huge horn over each eye and one above its nostrils, its head eight feet long and four feet high), and a fierce *Tyrannosaurus rex*.

The California Academy of Sciences in San Francisco has mounted a special "Jurassic" exhibit in the Natural History Museum. New York State Museum in Albany displayed fifteen lifelike dinosaur robots in a display that opened in July of 1993.

Utah Field House of Natural History, about twenty miles west of Dinosaur National Monument, bills itself as "Dinosaurland." It has fourteen life-size dinosaurs on a permanent display.

For a different kind of experience, a person might go to the Pine Butte Preserve and Guest Ranch in Montana. This 18,000-acre preserve and ranch are owned by the Nature Conservancy and the property includes a rich dinosaur bone bed. Visitors are invited to come and help excavate the site. The bone bed is a half-mile wide and two and a half miles long. Nearly every participant will, in fact, dig up genuine fossilized bones. Few of them are "articulated," connected at joints. Rather, the bones seem to be jumbled together across species. One theory is that the herd was wiped out by a volcanic eruption—the flesh of the beasts fried away by the heat of the explosion and the bones transported to the area by a mud slide.

From Science to Fantasy

So much for the serious displays. There are also a lot of "just fiction" displays. Flintstones' Bedrock City in South Dakota and Bedrock City in Arizona are both Flintstones theme parks. Prehistoric Gardens in Oregon has garishly painted dinosaurs in a recreated jungle, Land of Kong in Virginia has an odd assortment of vandalized dinosaur figures, and The Wheel Inn in Cabazon, California has a *Brontosaurus* named Dinny with a museum in its belly, a *Tyrannosaurus rex* with a slide down its tail, and a wooly mammoth.

Would-be Jurassic Parks include the Prehistoric Forest parks—one in Michigan and the other in Ohio, that have tram tours with crudely animated dinosaur figures, which emit recorded squawking sounds intended to frighten visitors. At the Ohio park, visitors are given toy M-16 rifles and told to "kill the monsters" if they attack.

The most elaborate park is likely to be one not yet open: Universal Studios theme parks is creating its own *Jurassic Park* exhibit.

Perhaps saddest of all, in my opinion, is the Dinosaur Garden in Ossineke, Michigan, which has a 60,000 pound life-size *Brontosaurus* nestled among pine trees and wild flowers. A staircase leads up into the figure's rib cage and there, one finds a pink and white striped shrine to Jesus Christ and the inscription, "the greatest heart."

5

Are Dinosaurs in the Bible?

Does the Bible even mention dinosaurs? Many believe it does.

Of course the word "dinosaur" does not appear in the Bible since the word was not in vocabulary until the 1800s. The Bible does speak, however, of creatures that we might recognize today as being dinosaurs.

"Tannin" is one of the Hebrew words that refers to dragon-like animals and great sea creatures (such as whales, giant squid, and marine reptiles). These references may be to dinosaurs. "Leviathan" is another term worthy of study.

Leviathan of the Deep

One of the oldest books in the Bible is the Book of Job. Scholars believe this book was written soon after the great Flood of Noah's time.

The entire chapter of Job 41 refers to a mysterious, large sea creature—identity unknown. Read this description and see if it doesn't sound amazingly like some of the descriptions today we read of *Plesiosaurs*.

Job is recording God's words to him:

> "Can you draw out Leviathan with a hook,
> Or snare his tongue with a line which you lower?

Can you put a reed through his nose,
Or pierce his jaw with a hook?
Will he make many supplications to you?
Will he speak softly to you?
Will he make a covenant with you?
Will you take him as a servant forever?
Will you play with him as with a bird,
Or will you leash him for your maidens?
Will your companions make a banquet of him?
Will they apportion him among the merchants?
Can you fill his skin with harpoons,
Or his head with fishing spears?
Lay your hand on him;
Remember the battle—
Never do it again!
Indeed, any hope of overcoming him is false;
Shall one not be overwhelmed at the sight of him?
No one is so fierce that he would dare stir him up.
Who then is able to stand against Me?
Who has preceded Me, that I should pay him?
Everything under heaven is Mine.

"I will not conceal his limbs,
His mighty power or his graceful proportions.
Who can remove his outer coat?
Who can approach him with a double bridle?
Who can open the doors of his face,
With his terrible teeth all around?
His rows of scales are his pride,
Shut up tightly as with a seal;
One is so near another
That no air can come between them;
They are joined one to another,
They stick together and cannot be parted.
His sneezings flash forth light,
And his eyes are like the eyelids of the morning.
Out of his mouth go burning lights;

Sparks of fire shoot out.
Smoke goes out of his nostrils,
As from a boiling pot and burning rushes.
His breath kindles coals.
And a flame goes out of his mouth.
Strength dwells in his neck,
And sorrow dances before him.
The folds of his flesh are joined together;
They are firm on him and cannot be moved.
His heart is as hard as stone,
Even as hard as the lower millstone.
When he raises himself up, the mighty are afraid;
Because of his crashings they are beside themselves.
Though the sword reaches him, it cannot avail;
Nor does spear, dart, or javelin.
He regards iron as straw,
And bronze as rotten wood.
The arrow cannot make him flee;
Slingstones become like stubble to him.
Darts are regarded as straw;
He laughs at the threat of javelins.
His undersides are like sharp potsherds;
He spreads pointed marks in the mire.
He makes the deep boil like a pot;
He makes the sea like a pot of ointment.
He leaves a shining wake behind him;
One would think the deep had white hair.
On earth there is nothing like him.
Which is made without fear.
He beholds every high thing;
He is king over all the children of pride."

Job 41

Two Creatures Instead of One?

Some Bible scholars now put a break between verses 11 and 12 of that chapter, indicated by the space above. They believe that chapter 41 actually describes two creatures—

the first a sea-going creature, the latter a "king of the beasts" creature, which is very similar to our description of armored dinosaurs.

Note the specific characteristics of Leviathan:

- it is a water-going creature (caught by hook, reed, or line)
- it has a strong jaw
- it is powerful and virtually uncatchable
- it is very tough skinned

Note the specific characteristics of what may be the second creature in Job 41:

- it has powerful, graceful limbs
- it has terrible teeth "all around"
- it has rows of scales, close together so as to form an impenetrable outer coat
- it breathes fire
- it eats small stones as if they were short grass (perhaps gastroliths)
- it has "tight" flesh (not saggy or fat)
- it has great strength
- it is capable of raising itself up (indicating that it may very well have been capable of walking on two legs)
- it "crashes" (rather than "splashes")
- it cannot be killed with arrows, slings and stones, spears, darts, or javelins
- it is capable of swimming—causing a "boiling" of waters
- it leaves behind in the waters a slick inky residue that shines "white."

A number of dinosaurs may have fit this description, but one of the interesting things to note in Job is that Job tells us what paleontologists will **never** be able to tell us—

exactly how these ancient creatures may have behaved and what may have been their characteristics.

The Creature Called Behemoth

In Chapter 40 of Job, we also find a very special creature Job calls "behemoth."

Again, Job is relating God's words to him:

> "Look now at the behemoth, which I made along with you;
> He eats grass like an ox.
> See now, his strength is in his hips,
> And his power is in his stomach muscles.
> He moves his tail like a cedar;
> The sinews of his thighs are tightly knit.
> His bones are like beams of bronze,
> His ribs like bars of iron.
> He is the first of the ways of God;
> Only He who made him can bring near His sword.
> Surely the mountains yield food for him,
> And all the beasts of the field play there.
> He lies under the lotus trees,
> In a covert of reeds and marsh.
> The lotus trees cover him with their shade;
> The willows by the brook surround him.
> Indeed the river may rage,
> Yet he is not disturbed.
> He is confident, though the Jordan gushes into
> his mouth,
> Though he takes it in his eyes,
> Or one pierces his nose with a snare."
>
> (Job 40:15-24, NKJV)

What do we know of this creature?

- It enjoyed resting in the marsh under willow trees (also called lotus).
- Even flooded rivers didn't scare it, so it apparently was comfortable in water and around water.

- No one could trap it.
- It was strong and large boned, a genuine giant, with a tail like the trunk of a tree.
- It was so gentle that other animals in the forest and fields were comfortable dwelling near it.
- Its mouth was large, but it ate grass.

God says to Job that He made this creature as the "first of His ways" (verse 19), which is another way of saying the "greatest" or the "biggest" or the "king."

Now reread this passage with the visual image of a *Diplodocus* in mind! The image seems to fit perfectly.

Bible translators frequently footnote this chapter in Job as referring to a hippopotamus, or even an elephant, but neither creature has a tail like a cedar!

Could Dragons Have Been Dinosaurs?

"But," you may say, "I thought these creatures in Job were mythical—like dragons." Let's consider that possibility. Myths and legends around the world tell of dragon-like creatures, including very specific stories and illustrations in Africa, India, Europe, The Middle East, and the Orient. Dinosaur-like animals have been drawn, written about, or told about since the beginning of human history! The word "dragon" actually comes from Europe. Many of the descriptions in the legends about dragons actually sound more like dinosaurs, however.

Those who study myths and legends have concluded that legends are nearly always based on fact, not just pure imagination. The facts may have been distorted or certain aspects of a story magnified, but the core fact of the story is nearly always related to an actual instance or experience.

One of the oldest legends is about a hero named Gilgamesh, who lived in Sumer (part of the Babylonian empire).

The legend tells how he set off on a journey to a distant land, in order to cut down great cedar trees to be used in building his city. He set off with fifty volunteers and sure enough, they reached a forest of giant trees. They also discovered a huge reptile-like animal in the forest—an animal that ate trees and reeds. Gilgamesh killed the creature and cut off its head for a trophy.

A city in France, Nerluc, is named in honor of a slain dragon that supposedly had long, sharp pointed horns on its head, and was about the size of an ox. The description is very like that of a *Triceratops*.

A carving on the wall of the Grand Canyon looks very much like an upright *Edmontosaurus*.

An ancient Roman mosaic shows two long-necked sea dragons at war.

A Scandinavian legend tells of a reptile-like animal that was about the size of a cow. It has very short front legs, a very big jaw, and very large and strong back legs. Could this have been a *Tyrannosaurus*?

Dragons are mentioned as being "real" until the 1500s, although writers of that time call them extremely rare and relatively small. In fact, a scientist named Ulysses Aldrovandus claimed to have seen a small dragon in northern Italy in 1572. A farmer had killed it by knocking it on the head when it hissed at his oxen. The scientist measured the body, made a drawing of it, and had it mounted for a museum. It had a long neck, very long tail, and fat body—a description that fits numerous ancient reptile-like creatures, but none known today.

The foremost land of the dragon, of course, is China. The dragon is still considered a major symbol of power among Chinese people—it was the symbol of the emperor for centuries. Old Chinese legends tell of dragons being chased into the sea when the rice patties were made . . . of families keeping dragons as pets . . . and of dragons pulling royal chariots.

An Irish legend tells of a beast that had iron nails on its tail. The nail-like spikes pointed backwards. It's head was a little like that of a horse, and it had thick legs with claws. A *Stegosaurus* or *Kentrosaurus* perhaps?

In Africa and Arabia small flying reptiles are described in ancient literature. The creatures had snake-like bodies and bat-like wings. The Greek explorer Herodotus wrote of being shown piles of their back-bones and ribs in a canyon near Buto in Arabia. Aristotle wrote of creatures like these living in Ethiopia. Bats? Hardly. The creatures are described as being at least three feet long!

But Can Creatures Breathe Fire?

One of the foremost features of dragons is that they are capable of spewing fire from their mouths. "Surely," you say, "that puts them completely in the realm of fiction." Maybe not.

How exactly would you explain to someone who had never seen one, how a "lightning bug" has a tail that glows in the dark as the result of an electro-chemical reaction?

Modern man has no trouble accommodating the idea of an "electric eel" that can emit 650 volts—enough to kill a man.

Modern man has no trouble studying the "bombadeer beetle" that holds chemicals in separate pouches near its mouth and when frightened or attacked, is capable of mixing those chemicals to emit a spark that has a scorching temperature of 212 degrees Fahrenheit!

Isn't it possible that a larger creature also had the capacity to produce chemical heat and light?

Modern man is quick to label anything that cannot be observed as preposterous, and yet . . . we allow for so many "preposterous" allegations about dinosaurs.

Modern man is quick to relegate creatures such as dragons to the world of the imagination, and yet . . . we allow for so much "imagining" in our explanation of dinosaurs.

Modern man is quick to dismiss the idea of creatures that may once have lived, but for which we have no hard evidence, and yet . . . we readily allow for extinction and the idea that not all species alive on the earth today have been discovered or defined fully.

Dinosaurs may very well be mentioned in the Bible—just under a different name!

6

What We Don't Know About Dinosaurs–

What Has Changed As "Fact" Over The Years

For all that fossilized bones and tracks tell us, there is a great deal they *don't* tell us.

Very, very, *very* few dinosaur skeletons have been found in complete form. Most skeletons are quite incomplete—perhaps just a few bones. Furthermore, many of the bones found are damaged, crushed or bent, or in some way damaged by the dirt and rock surrounding them. In many cases, "bone beds" feature a variety of creatures, with all of their bones mixed together.

A number of the pictures we have of dinosaurs today have been created from just a single tooth or leg bone!

The speculation about the way dinosaurs looked and acted is just that—speculation. In this field of study, there are many guesses and very few facts.

Stop to think for a moment about the world 6,000 years from now, should the Lord not return by then. How might we be depicted by those who discovered our bones . . . if our bones were the only clues they had about our appearance and behavior? Would we be adorned with feathers, tiger-striped skin, brightly colored heads? Would future scientists know our posture, standard body temperature, or anything about the texture of our skin?

A Product of Man's Imagination

In many ways, it is man who has created the dinosaur as we know it today. While paleontologists may have excavated and reconnected fossilized bones, it is the imagination of man that has added flesh, action, and interaction. Painters and sculptors have shaped our vision of dinosaurs. That's an important fact to keep at the forefront of any discussion related to dinosaurs.

Artists, even more than scientists, have shaped our understanding of dinosaurs.

Here's a very brief "art history lesson" about dinosaurs, and the way man's imagination has impacted, and in some cases altered, scientific fact . . . .

In 1834, fossil hunter Gideon Mantell commissioned John Martin to create a scene involving *Iguanodon*, the dinosaur Mantell had described in 1825. The result was a mezzotint titled "The Country of the *Iguanodon*," showing three great reptiles struggling within a primeval setting. It was used in Mantell's book *Wonders of Geology* (1938).

Benjamin Waterhouse Hawkins was the most influential dinosaur artist in the 19th century. His prominence spans the time of the Darwinian evolutionary debates and the period during which the first remains of relatively complete dinosaurs were discovered. His recreations of the *Iguanodon, Megalosaurus* and *Hylaeosauru*—completed in 1854 for the Crystal Palace at Sydenham—are now considered quite inaccurate. Indeed, Hawkins knew they were inaccurate even at the time. Richard Owen, the paleontologist who coined the term dinosaur, advised Hawkins that his Iguanodon had too many toes. Hawkins replied that if they were corns, he could have removed them, but since they were toes, they would have to remain!

Hawkins is credited with mounting the first dinosaur skeleton for the Philadelphia Academy of Sciences in 1868—a *Hadrosaurus*—but again, he wasn't completely truthful in his presentation. Unable to obtain an actual skull, he cast an oversized iguana skull with jaws sufficiently large to accommodate the teeth that had been excavated, and he scaled a human collarbone to fit the analogous missing parts of the skeleton.

Error compounded error. A popular book in the 1860s was Louis Figuier's book *The Earth Before the Deluge.* Edouard Riou was asked to provide illustrations for two scenes related to dinosaurs. His illustrations resemble greatly the models Hawkins had sculpted the previous decade.

Charles R. Knight worked with paleontologist Edward Drinker Cope in the late 1890s and they produced what many believe to be the 19th century's most beautiful dinosaur paintings. Unfortunately, there were hardly any fossils attributed to the *Laelaps* and *Agathaumas* depicted! The beautiful crest of horns in his *Agathaumas* painting is utter speculation—no skull had been discovered at that time!

Yet, it was Knight's depictions, produced largely from imagination, that became the basis for many of the early movie dinosaurs, particularly those in the 1925 version of *The Lost World.*

Zdenek Burian produced 381 dinosaur-themed oil paintings, most of them painted in the 1930s and 1940s. He also painted 114 watercolors on prehistory subjects and produced more than 15,000 illustrations. He claimed to be influenced by Knight's expert renderings!

It was a mural of the "Age of Reptiles" that won Rudolph Zallinger the 1949 Pulitzer Prize for painting. The mural was painted for the Yale University Peabody Museum's Great Hall. It is sixteen feet tall and 110 feet long—seventy-five feet of which is devoted to dinosaurs. The dinosaurs are painted in vivid hues that immediately capture one's attention. Zallinger, of course, had no idea what colors dinosaurs were. He later chuckled when he found paleontologists referring to his work as being an accurate coloration of dinosaurs.

Over the years, scientists, too, have dramatically altered their understanding of dinosaurs, both their appearance and their behavior. Very often they have "switched opinions" based on one part of one bone.

Did They Live in Swamps or on Prairies?

Diplodocus, a large plant-eater, had a nostril on the top of its head. Originally, scientists thought this dinosaur must have spent most of its time in water or swamps and may have been something of a snorkeler. They conjectured that an animal that large could not have spent its life walking on dry land. Later findings revealed that the creature had legs that could easily support its body, and that the bones of its feet seem to have allowed for cushions of flesh on the bottom—feet suitable for walking on hard ground, not swamp bottoms. Furthermore, its lung capacity was so small that immersion in deep water would likely have caused a pressure too great for it to breathe.

One stretch of Wyoming, a swath about a mile wide, has been called the "vegetative Pompeii" of the dinosaur world. This area has been studied in depth by Smithsonian Institution paleobotanist Scott Wing and his colleagues, who envision a terrain that was a sea of waist-high ferns, dotted with tiny palm trees and shrubs.

Paleobotanists are concluding that the landscape the dinosaurs roamed may very well have been mostly dry, with only sparse clumps of trees—more like a modern savanna than a bayou.

Did They Walk on Two Legs or Four?

For decades, scientists thought all dinosaurs walked on four legs, like the "lizards" they supposedly were.

In excavating thirty-nine *Iguanadons* in a mine in Belgium, scientists decided that the creature didn't walk on four legs at all, but on two.

For the next thirty years, the exact stance of dinosaurs was debated hotly. R.T. Byrd was the finder of the Glen Rose tracks in the Paluxy River, a find regarded as definitive proof that some dinosaurs, at least, walked on two legs.

Still, other dinosaurs thought to have walked on two legs now appear to have walked "mostly" on four, with the capability of raising themselves up occasionally on two legs to reach for top branches of trees.

How Many Were There?

We do not know how many dinosaur varieties roamed the earth. Some bone beds seem to point toward there being thousands of a particular species. On the other hand, only eleven skeletons of the *Tyrannosaurus rex* have ever been discovered and all of them have come from the western interior region of the United States.

The total number of dinosaurs that lived on the earth at any one time has never been fully calculated, nor is it likely to be.

How dense or how pervasive were herds of dinosaurs? We simply do not know.

What Did They Sound Like?

Some scientists have assumed that the dinosaurs moved in herds and communicated by sending low calls to each other (similar to way elephants communicate today). Jack Horner, for example, has discovered a group of dinosaurs called *Lambeosaurs* that had a large hollow chamber within their skulls, above their nasal cavity and up past their forehead. Horner has simulated the shape of this cavity in a laboratory, using plastic tubing. He has found that it produces a loud, low-frequency sound that could travel for miles.

The *Camarasaurus* was a large plant-eater. It had two very large holes in its skull, separated by a ridge of bone. This bone configuration may have accommodated very large nostrils, and perhaps even an appendage—something like a short elephant's trunk. This may have allowed the dinosaur to make bellowing and tooting noises.

But exactly what kind of sounds did dinosaurs make, and what caused them to bellow, toot, or roar? We simply do not know.

A Wide Variety of Sizes . . .

We tend to think of all dinosaurs in any one particular species as being the same size. Reptiles, of course, continue to grow as long as they are alive. Some turtles alive today, for example, are massive. They are estimated to be as many as three hundred years old!

Most *Velociraptor* skeletons are about six feet tall, the size of an average man—except for one. A *Velociraptor* has been found in Utah that was twenty feet tall. It's called *Utahraptor*.

One of the things scientists don't know for sure is whether certain species changed shape as they grew. Human babies today, as an example, are born with heads that are quite large in proportion to their bodies. Over the lifespan of a human being, the **body**—not the head—is the part that grows and the entire proportion of the body changes—including the size and relationship of various bones to one another. Could the same thing be true of dinosaurs? We don't know.

Which Fossil is the Oldest?

That's a debate right now. Some say the oldest dinosaur bones are those from the neck and skull of an *Herrarasaurus* found in Argentine. Others claim it is the *Lagosuchus*, the "rabbit crocodile." This creature was about the size of a chicken— with long legs and feet that would have helped it leap like a rabbit, and a strong long tail like a crocodile's. It's neck, however, was long and capable of bending into a curve—something neither a rabbit nor a crocodile can do, but something dinosaurs *could* do. Scientists think it was a meat-eater because of its dagger-like teeth—something a rabbit doesn't have. Those who buy into evolution science see this creature as a possible "link" between the pre-mesozoic era and the age of dinosaurs. If that's the case, then in order for it to fit into the evolutionary column, it *must* be old.

Did Dinosaurs Migrate or Stay in One Location?

Scientists thought for years that dinosaurs were so slow and lumbering that they were born, lived, and died in a fairly short radius. Some now believe they may have migrated hundreds of miles in following climate changes and availability of foliage, likely in a north to south and south to north pattern.

Drooping or Proud Tails?

The original design of "dragging tails" for dinosaurs was replaced by the idea of "drooping tails," which was the prevailing opinion for a number of years (and which accommodated the thinking that a number of dinosaurs walked on two legs). Today, a number of scientists believe that even quadropeds may have held their tails straight out.

One Brain or Two?

Scientists have long noted that a number of large dinosaurs apparently had very small brain sizes, especially in comparison to their body size. Some now think that the large *Brachiosaurus* may have had a second brain located toward the rear of its body cavity.

T-Rex: A Case Study

The way thinking has changed about dinosaurs through the years can be applied specifically to *Tyrannosaurus rex*—perhaps the best known of all dinosaurs to our children.

For decades scientists also thought that *T-rex* walked upright with its tail dragging along the ground. Now, paleontologists believe that *T-rex*, like many dinosaurs, had a more birdlike carriage, with its head forward and its tail sticking out behind it.

T-rex was also thought at one time to be quite fast. Some even estimated he could run as fast as forty miles per hour. Now, scientists have concluded that since the creature's upper and lower leg bones are about equal in length, *T-rex* may have waddled like a duck—in a stooped-over position—and have been quite slow!

Was he really the fiercest dinosaur? Well, he certainly wasn't the largest by any means. *T-rex* was, at most, forty-feet long and twenty-feet high. Did he have the most powerful jaws? No. *Triceratops* has the strongest jaw found to date.

T-rex has long been considered a fearsome carnivore, quick to engage in battle. Some think now, however, that he may have scavenged for his food. They point to the creature's arms—only about the size of a human's. *T-rex* could not put its hands together, nor could it raise its arms to its mouth. This finding has led scientists to conclude that the animals got more of its meat from scavenging than from hunting and ripping apart animals.

Yet another group of scientists have concluded that *T-rex* was not a carnivore at all. They point to the fact that the creatures serrated teeth are serrated along the length of the tooth—rather than across the teeth—a pattern more consistent with creatures that strip bark, cane, and small branches from trees (rather than strip skin and flesh from a carcass). They also point toward the shallow embedding of the teeth in the jaw. The seven-to-eleven-inch-long teeth are embedded only two inches into the jaw. To rip through skin with lizard-like toughness, would take considerable strength and they conjecture that the teeth of a *T-rex* would have been more likely to be pulled from the jaw rather than be able to engage in such a task routinely!

Did *T-rex* look fierce? Probably so. That opinion hasn't changed. With a wide mouth and sixty teeth, each of which is about the length of the distance between a person's elbow and wrist, there's a lot to *avoid* about *T-rex*.

The fierce-looking *Tyrannosaurus rex* a waddling, slow, vegetarian? Hard to imagine—yet quite plausible!

What About the *Brontosaurus*?

Millions of people can describe for you the way a *Brontosaurus*—the great "thunder lizard"—looks. Unfortunately, none ever really existed—even though dinosaur books and museums have featured this giant sauropod for years.

The dinosaur body called *Brontosaurus* was discovered with its head missing. A scientist added a skull he found several miles away.

In actuality, the body of *Brontosaurus* is today known as the skeleton of a *Diplodocus*. The skull was that of an *Apatosarus*. In sum, there *is* no *Brontosaurus* species.

What about *Stegosaurus*?

Most children can quickly identify a *Stegosaurus*—the dinosaur with the protruding, boney plates running along the ridge of its back. Scientists, however, disagree about the function and purpose of those big leaf-shaped plates of bone. The plates have a number of hollow tubes that may have held blood vessels. Some scientists think the blood worked like water in the radiator of a car to cool off the creature on hot days. Others think the bones were strictly ornamental to attract mates. Still others think the plates may actually have moved—like flaps—and were designed to protect the *Stegosaurus* from attack. Furthermore, some think there were two rows of parallel plates, others believe there was only one.

What About *Triceratops*?

Scientists once envisioned fierce battles between *T-rex* and *Triceratops*. It appears more likely now that the *Triceratops* horns were used more for engaging in sexual and territorial dominance battles within its own species.

A Wide Variety of Interpretations

Other would-be facts about dinosaurs also lend themselves to differing interpretations. For example, the *Pachycephalosaurus* was apparently a hard-headed dinosaur that had a dome-shaped skull that was ten inches thick. Some scientists speculate this armored plate was used in ritual head-butting contests among fellow carnivores—others conclude that the creature was a herbivore and used his hard head to butt against trees to knock down ripe fruit!

The Purpose for Claws and Sharp Teeth

A basic assumption has been made for decades about sharp teeth and claws which may, or may not, be true. Scientists have assumed that sharp teeth and claws were used for ripping apart flesh—skin, sinew, muscle, bones, and so forth.

In a number of cases, however, scientists also have not yet determined if a bone *is* a horn, or a spike, or a claw! That's been an issue since the first fossil find. The tooth-shaped structure that Mantell depicted as an *Iguanodon* "horn" and which he positioned on the tip of the creature's snout, was later identified as a thumb!

Not all animals today that have sharp claws and teeth consume flesh. A number of bird species, for example, use their claws and sharp beaks for breaking into melons and nuts. The same goes for the Giant Panda, the large Australian fruit bat, and some bears and apes.

Several discrepancies have been noted about supposedly meat-eating dinosaurs.

First, if they indeed chewed through muscle and bone, their teeth should show significant wear, and occasionally be broken off. The intact jaws of sharp-toothed adult dinosaurs don't show this wear. The tips of the teeth found, in fact, show almost no wear and the delicate edge serrations of the teeth can be clearly seen in almost perfect condition. Only rarely is a tooth found missing in a supposed carnivore jaw, even though the teeth sit in a shallow manner in the jawbone. Broken teeth are even rarer.

Second, spiked or spinney "carnivores" actually show little wear or breakage of these appendages, which are usually quite delicate. The *Spinosaurus*, for example, has thin spines that stood straight up and were about six and a half-feet high. Reason tells us that if this animal engaged in fierce fighting with other animals for its food—or even if it scavenged for food inside the remains of larger herbivores—some of these spines should be broken, bent, or be missing. That isn't the case.

Third, a number of dinosaurs, especially those similar to *Dilophasaurus* (which had two high, paper-thin bone crests) should show some wear to their fragile head bones if these animals were rooting around inside dead dinosaurs, greedily vying for and tearing apart bone and sinew. If such an animal truly was a fighter—winning its meat in battles against other animals—these crests should definitely show occasional breakage or wear in the fossils. They don't.

Even if dinosaurs did eat meat, there's not a lot of evidence to support the idea that they hunted and killed for it.

In one notable instance, we see evidence of communal eating of a plant-eating dinosaur by a group of meat-eaters. The remains of eight *Deinonychus* were found clustered around one large plant-eater called *Tenontosaurus*. What scientists cannot tell, however, is how these *Deinonychus* attacked, or even if they did. Perhaps they were simply eating the remains of a creature that had died.

The fact is, we simply do not *know* with any degree of certainty that carnivores were truly carnivores, and even if they were, that they fought among themselves or against herbivores in the Early Earth.

If dinosaurs didn't use their horns or sharp teeth for fighting or defending, what may have been their purpose?

Head horns may have been used something like a forklift, for rooting, turning over plants, and poking through fallen trees. The boney-plated heads of some dinosaurs may have been used for butting up against tall trees in order to knock out ripe fruit, or to turn over rocks.

Finally, consider the nature of meat-eaters on the earth today—especially those that hung for their food. They tend to be smooth, sleek creatures. Tigers, lions, and wolves do **not** have any aspect of their beings that might be considered extraneous, fragile, or easily broken!

Furthermore, the "reptiles" of today are not considered fierce hunters by any means. For the most part, they are defensive creatures. Their mainstay diet tends to be insects and rodents—not creatures significantly larger than themselves!

Cold or Warm Blooded?

Perhaps the major shift in scientific positions over the years has been whether dinosaurs were warm or cold-blooded.

In the past, scientists saw dinosaurs as large, cumbersome, and cold-blooded. Today, scientists know that some dinosaurs were quite small, agile, and warm-blooded.

Some paleontologists have concluded that some dinosaurs were warm-blooded by comparing the size of adults in the species to the size of their young at birth. A rapid growth pattern is typical of the fast metabolism found in warm-blooded creatures.

Other scientists are now concluding that dinosaurs were **neither** strictly warm blooded nor cold-blooded, but something entirely unique—with a metabolism not found in the world today. In studying very thin slices of bones, they have found that early in a dinosaur's life, the growing bones were filled with many tiny blood vessels—a sign of a rapid, warm-blooded metabolism very much like that of a bird. In adult specimens, however, the number of bone vessels in the bones dropped dramatically, suggesting that at some point in its life, it had switched gears and adopted the slower metabolism that is more typical of a cold-blooded reptile. This ability to switch may have been partially the factor that led them to grow to such enormous sizes. Staying cool is a much more difficult thing to do when you are a large warm-blooded creature than when you are small or cold-blooded.

Still others are concluding that they **were** cold-blooded, but could do what warm-blooded creatures do.

The main objection to migration was that cold-blooded reptiles would require too much energy to travel such distances. Recent studies show that even though reptiles are cold-blooded, they can also travel hundreds and even thousands of miles (as in the case of the leatherback turtles, which weigh up to 625 pounds and yet travel some 2,000 miles from the waters of southern Alaska to the coastal islands of Central America. Scientists have concluded that reptiles are able to take advantage of a principle they call "gigantothermy"—which states, in a nutshell, that while large reptiles are slower to cool and slower to get warm, once cool or warm, they tend to stay that way (just as a well-insulated house).

Still others claim that both cold and warm-blooded dinosaurs roamed the earth—and that from only one to three percent were warm blooded.

Bird or Reptile, or Both?

It seems increasingly that dinosaurs are being linked to birds. Indeed, the two share many features such as bone structure, warm bloodedness, and of course, nesting behavior.

Pluck a bird today of its feathers and you have a strange-looking creature not unlike many illustrations we have of dinosaur fossils. In converse, it is interesting to imagine ancient dinosaurs covered with feathers. Perhaps they were more bird than lizard?

Dinosaurs seem to have treated their young more like birds than reptiles. At one time, scientists concluded that since dinosaurs laid their eggs in nests, as crocodiles and other lizards we know today, that they let their young fend on their own (as reptiles do today). Evidence appears fairly certain now, however, that at least some species nurtured their young while they were in the nest, similar to the way that birds do.

For years, evolution scientists stated that reptiles evolved into birds. In other words, birds didn't exist during the time of reptiles, or before them. The thinking also was that birds were reptiles that traded in scales for feathers, lost their teeth, and kept their claws.

And then they found *Archaeopteryx*—again, a major mystery to scientists. The skeleton of this creature was found in almost perfect condition between two layers of a smooth rock. At the time the fossil was found, however, scientists thought all dinosaurs that "age" were cold-blooded. But this creature obviously had feathers. Why would a creature need feathers to keep it warm if it was cold blooded? Was *Archaeopteryx*—which means ancient wing—a feathered dinosaur or the first bird?

Now, scientists have evidence in the fossil record of birds that are supposedly older than those of dinosaurs and reptiles. Furthermore, species of living birds have been found with teeth. And there is **no** evidence in the fossil record of creatures having both scales and feathers, or of scales becoming feathers.

A Lot Still to Learn

Yes, there's a great deal we *don't* know about dinosaurs, and some things we'll probably never know. For example, we have no idea what color dinosaurs were. We assume they were dull greens and browns because that's the way we see reptiles today. Might they have been brightly colored and patterned as one paleontologist, Robert Bakker, thinks?

The eight foot "sail" on the back of the *Spinosaurus* is still a great mystery.

The long claws and teeth on a *Baryonyx* are also a mystery. This creature apparently fed on fish, the way crocodiles do, so why did it need large curved hook-like claws?

The fact is . . .

No matter how learned we become, we will never unlock all of the secrets of God's creation.

That is a realization that should not dismay, but cause wonder. Scientific research is a wonderful thing. Inquiry into our present and past should be encouraged, not discouraged. We need more Christian scientists and more Christian technologists who can help us adapt scientific findings toward the betterment of our lives.

Still, we will never know it all. The universe is a vast domain and our God an infinite God. That means that we will always have the "unknown" to deal with.

We need to face up to the fact that mystery will always be associated with God, and that mystery is not only acceptable, but something to be embraced.

- God is knowable, but we will never have Him figured out.
- God is approachable, but we must never approach Him with anything but awe.
- God is accessible, but we must never think we are in a position to manipulate or control Him.

- God's ways are discoverable, but we must always recognize that His ways are "higher" than our ways. (Isaiah 55:9)

In the end, we don't **need** to know everything there is to know about dinosaurs.

In the end, all we *really* need to know is that we have a relationship with the Lord Jesus Christ, and through Him, the Creator of dinosaurs.

7

Dinosaurs and Evolution Science

The one fact that all Christian parents must face today is this:

Dinosaurs are nearly always used in our public schools to teach evolution science. The general teachings are these:

1. Dinosaurs are prehistoric—they lived long before the Bible (or any other book) was written, and long before man existed.
2. Dinosaurs exist because they evolved out of the sea as "reptiles." Only very small dinosaurs survived a major catastrophe that hit the earth about 65 million years ago, and they subsequently evolved into the mammals we know today.
3. There was a time when the earth was inhabited *only by giant reptiles and birds.*

Evolution, however, is not a "fact," as many would have us believe. It is a *theory.*

Theories Arise from Belief Systems

All theories arise from a belief system. That's not a fact that many scientists are willing to admit openly, but the truly great scientists readily confess that the seed ideas for their theories generally arise from their belief system, values, and intuitive understanding of the world.

Is there a metaphysical belief system underlying the theory of evolution?

Yes. The foremost influence is probably found in the philosophy of Hinduism. Hinduism states that mankind is in the process of moving from lower levels of consciousness to higher levels of consciousness. This process occurs, of course, over a long long period of time—and through a number of different "life forms" experienced by any one entity. All creatures are on an evolving journey and thus, all creatures are equal in value. There is no judgment or sin in Hinduism—only things that impede a person's movement from a lower to higher level of awareness and understanding. No outside force is involved in the process. It is the "nature" of a creature to evolve in consciousness according to its own timetable and internalization of experiences.

Erasmus Darwin, the grandfather of Charles Darwin, lived in the 1700s and was part of a group of people who sought to explain away the idea that God had created all life. He was the head of the Lunar Society, a group that met monthly at the full moon. This particular group arose in part during the post-French-revolution era. In France, the revolution had included an overthrow of all Church authority. In England, the tactic became not an overthrow of the Church, which was largely a political organization, but a refutation of the "authority" given to the Bible. Erasmus Darwin wrote a great deal that served as the foundation for Charles Darwin's subsequent writings.

It was when Charles Darwin became disgruntled with the Church on a personal level, that he began to explore more fully the ideas put forth by his grandfather.

Note the sequence in both of these men's lives. They did not begin with a body of factual **evidence** first, and attempt to formulate a theory to accommodate it. Both Darwins were consumed with an **idea** first, and that idea was firmly rooted in rebellion against God, the Church, and the Bible.

In much of science, men and women see **evidence** first. A reaction takes place. Bread turns moldy. Repeatedly. In similar conditions. "What causes the mold?" they ask. They put forth a possible explanation and attempt to test it.

Or, two chemicals seem to act a specific way when put together. Or, natural signs seem to reappear consistently. An explanation is sought. A theory—or idea—is put forth as to how this happens and under what repeatable, observable conditions.

The theory of evolution did not begin that way. It began when men took a look at the Bible and said, "I don't believe that. What might have happened if God had **not** been responsible for the creation of the world?"

Evolution was put forth as a theory **before** the first ancient dinosaur fossil was found . . . **before** geological formation studies had been adequately tested . . . **before** any definitive conclusions could be drawn related to the capability of any simple life form to mutate spontaneously into something higher and more complex.

And yet, evolution has come to be regarded as the only credible world view. Most Americans, if asked in a man-on-the-street-style interview, would probably state that:

- The theory of evolution has been proven to be true.
- Those who believe in The Creation account of the Bible are naive, ill-informed, and dangerous (in that they are attempting to push science back to the Dark Ages).

These ideas aren't limited to the common man. They have been published as such by the late science writer Isaac Asimov and also in an official document titled "Science and Creationism—A View from the National Academy of Science."

In California, educators have proposed a "Science Framework" for K-12 instruction. It states that Darwin's "descent with modification" is the central life principle that must be taught, and that evolution is the only theory that should be presented to children.

The fact is, however, that the theory of evolution has **not** been proven fully. In fact, the only aspects of the theory that seem to remain credible today are the ideas of "survival of the fittest" and "extinction." Creation scientists actually have no qualms with those two aspects of the evolutionary theory. Strong, numerous, and healthy life forms do tend to overcome and depopulate weak, scattered, and sick life forms. Species do become extinct.

Other facets of the theory of evolution have been dramatically overthrown or argued vigorously by the scientific community. It's the educational and political world that is slow to catch up!

Let's look at several of the ideas associated with evolution that simply do not make sense to a logical person and which cannot be proven in any definitive manner.

Evolution Science: The Big Bang

This idea states that an initial massive explosion sent matter hurling through time and space into the order we see it today. In other words, chaos created order. This approach has several serious problems. First, there is no observable, repeatable evidence that explosions of any kind **create order.** If anything, they result in destruction of that which has been created, and they cause disorder.

The theory is contradictory to the second law of thermodynamics, which states that things are moving from a state of order to disorder over time. This is a law observable in numerous examples all around us—cars rust out, bodies wear out, stars burn out, even the sun glows with less intensity.

Furthermore, random events may take on a semblance of "order" over time in a person's perspective, but that order is perceived, not actual. Rarely do random events result in predictability. The very terms are incompatible.

And finally, nobody has ever figured out where space and matter—the "substance" of the Big Bang—came from originally.

Evolution Science: The Long-Time-Dead Factor

Science relies on repeatability and observation. Scientists monitor reactions or observe results with an eye toward recording what is repeatable and predictable, and which changes are not only observable but statistically significant.

Evolution takes a very different tact. It calls for **long** periods of time—time periods that span not only more than one life or one generation, but thousands and millions of years. Thus, **no** acts of evolution can be or ever have been replicated or observed directly. All of them must be inferred from dead matter (fossils, rock layers, and so forth).

In many ways, the idea of evolution has been positioned so that it **cannot** be proved. Yet, it is held as not only provable, but proven, by many people.

Critics of evolution hold that if the **processes** are true, then they should be reproducible within a time span that can be observed and documented, at least on a partial or minute scale. This has never been done.

A great deal of research is presently going in that very direction. Here is what Time magazine wrote:

"UCLA paleobiologist J. William Schopf reported finding fossilized imprints of a thriving microbial community sandwiched between layers of rock that is 3.5 billion years old. This, along with other evidence, shows that life was well established only a billion years after the earth's formation, a much faster evolution than previously thought. Life did not arise under calm, benign conditions, as once assumed, but under the hellish skies of a planet racked by volcanic eruptions and menaced by comets and asteroids. In fact, the intruders from outer space may have delivered the raw materials necessary for life. So robust were the forces that gave rise to the first living organisms that it is entirely possible, many researchers believe, that life began not once, but several times before it finally 'took' and colonized the planet.

"The notion that life arose quickly and easily has spurred scientists to attempt a truly presumptuous feat: they want to create life—real life—in the lab. What they have in mind is not some monster like Frankenstein's, pieced together from body parts and jolted into consciousness by lightning bolts, but something more like the molecule in that thimble-size test tube at the Scripps Research Institute. They want to turn the hands of time all the way back to the beginning and create an entity that approximates the first, most primitive living thing. This ancient ancestor, believes Gerald Joyce, whose laboratory came up with the Scripps molecule, may have been a simpler, sturdier precursor of modern RNA, which, along with the nucleic acid DNA, its chemical cousin, carries the genetic code in all creatures great and small.

"Some such molecule, Joyce and other scientists believe, arose in the shadowy twilight zone where the distinction between living and nonliving blurs and finally disappears. The precise chemical wizardry that caused it to pass from one side to the other remains unknown."

(*Time*, October 11, 1993, pages 70-71)

Notice the number of times the word "believe" and "may" have been used in this brief quote.

The fact is, when one is dealing with supposedly **billions** of years of time . . . one is limited to "believing" things. Nothing can be proven in a definitive fashion, not a precise moment, not an understanding of precise conditions, and not even a precise process.

Evolution Science: Eras and Dating Methods

The Age of Dinosaurs supposedly spanned the length and breadth of the Mesozoic Era. That era is divided by evolution scientists into three major periods:

- The Triassic Period
  (245-213 million years ago)
- The Jurassic Period
  (213-144 million years ago)
- The Cretaceous period
  (144-65 million years ago)

Where did these periods and dates originate?

In the 1700's, James Hutton and Charles Lyell proposed a system of life development that "predated" known history. The Geologic Column or Geologic Time Scale was produced by Lyell, who also wrote the *Antiquity of Man*, a book in which he conjectured that man as a species was much older than believed at that time.

Lyell's system of geological dating was based on what he observed in a nearby formation that showed layers of rock in stratas. The **dates** (such as 225 million years ago) were placed on the column by Lyell as a guess! He did not have evidence to back up his dating on the column, other than his own theory of "uniformitarianism" that suggested that the earth has experienced a uniform rate of volcanic activity over time, that the earth's atmosphere has remained constant, and that the chemical proportions of the earth have remained the same from the beginning of time to the present.

Many people have come to regard the Geological Column as fact.

From its outset and remaining to this day, it is a **theory.**

The Geological Column was Lyell's opinion that the layers of the earth (stratas) corresponded to evolutionary levels of life. The dating on the scale was strictly arbitrary—in other words, "in his opinion."

The stratas that Lyell noted are **not** universal. In fact, they are not found precisely as he constructed them anywhere on the earth. The fossil record does not match up precisely with either the stratas or in the relationship advocated among species.

And yet . . . a number of scientists still continue to date fossils based upon their position on Lyell's chart!

Radiometric Dating. In an attempt to "date" materials, two radiometric methods were developed. The first is the uranium-lead method, the second is the potassium-argon method. Both assume an even breakdown of matter over time, a breakdown that is uniform because conditions impacting these elements are supposedly uniform.

Neither method, however, provides consistent results.

The same lunar rocks subjected to several test periods were classified as being 4.6, 4.8, 5.6, and 8.2 **billion** years old. That's a discrepancy in age of more than 3.6 billion years— from just one rock sample!

Fossils are dated usually by the radiometric dating of the **rocks** immediately surrounding those life forms. Thus, material supposedly takes on the age in which it was encapsulated. Lava taken from a volcano known to have erupted in the period 1800-1801, was dated as being **millions** of years old. Any creatures "captured" in such a lava flow, however, are not necessarily that old!

Carbon Dating. A different form of dating is used to date organic material. The assumption has been made that all living things contain carbon-14. By measuring the ratio of carbon-14 to carbon-12 in a fairly elaborate formula, scientists measure the "half-life" of an organism.

The method hinges on one basic principle: carbon-14 has remained constant in the earth's atmosphere for the entire history of the earth. That simply isn't true. Scientists have found trees that were apparently alive during a comet shower. The carbon-14 level in those trees doubled in one year. Solar flares also change the amount of carbon-14 in the atmosphere.

The assumption is also made that the initial ratio of carbon-14 to carbon-12 in plants and animals has always been similar to what it is today. Maybe not.

The main thing to know, however, is that this method is also not always accurate.

Using this method, freshly killed seals have been dated to be 1300 years old. **live** mollusks have been dated as being 2300 years old!

Evolution Science: Life From Non-Living Material

Evolution calls for the "spontaneous generation" of life from nonliving material. Some evolution scientists state that a lightning bolt hit a pond, causing normal chemical reactions to mutate and begin to replicate in a living fashion. Darwin wrote about a "warm little pond" that had a rich brew of organic chemicals that over eons of time, produced the first simple organisms.

The observation all around us, however, is that life comes from life. Our world has no examples of nonliving materials producing living material.

The problem is confounded by those who do not believe that we have yet discovered the most basic of "elements" that comprise the life formula. Is there something even beyond RNA and DNA? Is there something smaller than a quark? Is there an entire pattern of reactions and entities that might exist because we do not yet have the technology or understanding to explore that hidden universe—in the same way that men and women a thousand years ago had no concept of a human cell, or for that matter, the concept of a virus that could invade a human cell? Very possibly!

Even if man concludes that life can spring from nonliving material—how can we truly know whether an even more basic **living** material exists that has not yet been identified? We don't. We can't. Ultimately, we are back to what we choose to **believe.**

Furthermore, even should nonliving matter result in matter that reproduces . . . does that explain the fullness of life as we human beings know it?

Hardly.

Who can tell how nerve cells create emotions? Who can know how brain cells produce innovative ideas? Movement and replication don't define the human soul.

In a nutshell, evolution is based on the ideas that Chance + Time + Raw Chemical Material = a complex design of life.

The common person, looking around at his own life and the world he knows, would probably never draw that conclusion. Life may be subject to the effects of chance and time . . . but time and chance don't produce life. Life flows from life.

Evolution Science: Mutations Result in Improvement

Evolution takes the position that mutations over time, subjected to the forces of natural selection, result in an improved quality of life and a new species.

This hasn't been proven in any laboratory.

Rather, when species are bombarded with chemicals, energy, light, heat, and other mutation-causing "treatments," the mutations that result do not **improve** the quality of life for that species. The creatures, instead, appear impaired, broken, sick, weak, deformed, less mobile, less able to replicate, and less intelligent.

Furthermore, mutations have not been shown to result in new species. Very often, mutants are rendered sterile! If anything, the natural selection process ensures that mutants **don't** replicate!

Evolution calls for these mutations over time to result in more and bigger species.

In reality, we have fewer and smaller species on the earth today. Some scientists believe that literally billions of species have been "subtracted" from the initial creation, or have been eliminated through the millennia.

Finally, if mutations are the backbone of evolutionary thought . . . the assumption seems likely that **all** life forms should be evolving to some degree at all times, possibly changing a great deal, but certainly changing a *little bit* over thousands of years. If some creatures mutate and change, surely all do, to some degree! Again, this hasn't been proven. Scientists see **no** change in ants, mosquitos, or praying mantis species, for example—even over thousands of years!

Evolution Science: A Common Ancestry

One of the best-known illustrations of evolution science is that of the "tree of life."

This tree assumes a common ancestry for all creatures and presupposes that all species are "linked" together by mutations.

Despite decades of research and thousands of fossil finds, evolutions have been unable to devise any truly workable scheme of a common ancestry linking the various main types of dinosaurs. Each basic kind of dinosaur (whether *Carnosaur, Ornithopod, Sauropod, Stegosaur,* and so forth) is unique and widely different from the others. There are no links that place them on the same evolutionary "tree."

The same is true of the *Pterosaurs* (the flying reptiles). No trace has been found of a common ancestor. For example, no fossil reptile has been found with only rudimentary wings or "wing stumps."

The dinosaurs appear abruptly in the fossil record, fully developed, without any proof of intermediate stages.

In a recent issue of *Discover* magazine (September 1993), Robert Bakker explores the topic of "Jurassic Sea Monsters" and concludes that the "extinction schedules for *ichthyosaurs* and *pliosaurs* were the reverse of those for land ecosystems— the top predators were least vulnerable" (pg. 82). Furthermore, he concludes that while the body forms of Cretaceous and Jurassic long-necked *Plesiosaurs* look identical—with fore and aft flippers, and proportions of neck and torso, shoulders and hips the same—they are in fact quite different.

He cites the example of an African spotted hyena and the fact that it looks like a tall version of the African hyena dog. The skull anatomy of the two mammals, however, show that the hyena dog is a genuine member of the dog family—a close kin of the jackal, wolf, and coyote. The spotted hyena, on the other hand is related to cats, civets, and mongooses. In like manner, the two species of *plesiosaur* are different.

This is not to say at all that Bakker is ready to overthrow basic tenets of evolution. His argument, rather, is that sea-monster evolution follows something of an inverse pattern to land-based evolution. The point I find intriguing is that the principles of the evolutionary theory are still being tested, still being altered, and scientists are still unable to categorize all creatures along its rather elaborate timetables.

Evolutionists frequently confront creationists on the point of specificity. One hears often, "Creation isn't a science. It can't be proven." The evolutionists fail to point out, however, that the so-called provable points of "evolution" are still very much unproven.

According to the basic tenets of evolution, small and lesser dinosaurs should be found in the "more ancient" stratas than the giant, more complex dinosaurs. The fossils, however, don't support that expectation. The largest, most numerous, and widest variety of dinosaurs are found in the more ancient Jurassic strata, not in the 'later' Cretaceous strata! The Jurassic-era dinosaurs include *Apatosaurus, Diplodocus and Brachiosaurus*. No smaller or "partially developed" versions of these creatures have been found. They appear abruptly and seemingly from nowhere in the fossil record.

The first person to coin the term dinosaurs, Sir Richard Owen, former head of the Natural History Museum in London, called the creatures the "crown of reptilian creation." He suggested that they provided more evidence for

DE-evolution than for evolution—that they gave rise to a theory of degenerative changes over time from their original magnificence to the lowly reptiles we have on earth today.

One of the net effects of evolution science is a belief that all life forms are equal. In *The Cosmic Connection*, Carl Sagan writes, "Spiders and salamanders, salmon and sunflowers are equally our brothers and sisters."

That is tantamount, in my opinion, to the worship of creation. When all of the created order is held as equally valuable, then man is reduced to being a creature among creatures—not the creature authorized by God to have dominion over, encourage the multiplication of, and oversee the reproduction of other creatures.

The Christian approach to man's position in the universe is not as centrist as many evolution scientists seem to believe. The biblical approach is not that man is the center of the universe . . . but that God is. The creation science approach says that:

- God is infinite, man is finite.
- God is creator, man is created.
- Many orders were created by God . . . man's position is *a little lower than the angels* and over the rest of living things on the earth. (See Hebrews 2:9.)
- Man has the responsibility for governing, naming, and controlling the rest of the living creation.
- Animals, conversely do **not** have this responsibility for other animals or for man!

The Apostle Paul warned believers against worshipping the creature more than the Creator. (Romans 1:25) That is very often the tendency of those who see animals and plants as being equal to man.

Evolution Science and the Demise of the Dinosaurs

A display banner in the Royal Tyrrell Museum in Canada says it all:

Dinosaurs are dead. All of them. Something happened about 64 million years ago that ended their line.

To the left of the banner is an alcove that lists the names of the species that have been discovered—all the way to the *Leptoceratops*, which many paleontologists believe was the last remaining species. What happened to the dinosaurs?

The list of possibilities made through the years has been a long one:

- Disease killed them.
- The weather changed.
- The atmosphere changed.
- A meteor hit the earth and they suffocated from the dust it caused.
- The mammals ate their eggs.

Or in the words of one three-year-old boy, "They just killed each other and ate each other up."

In all, nearly sixty theories have been put forth over the years as to why the dinosaurs disappeared from the earth.

Both "hot" and "cold" theories have been developed. Hot theories involve volcanoes and cold theories involve ice caps and ice ages. In evolution science, the friction of hot and cold accounts for divisions in land masses and the shift of continents.

There are only two universal facts about which all scientists seem to agree:

- The death of the dinosaurs on the earth was rapid and complete; it happened in a fairly short period of time.

97

- The extinction of the dinosaurs happened around the world at the same time; whatever caused the dinosaurs to disappear was a world-wide event.

The foremost theory in the scientific community to-day—one first proposed in 1980—says that an asteroid hit the earth's surface with such impact that material was hurled back up into the upper atmosphere with such volume that the sun was obscured for at least a three-month period of time and possibly as long as three years.

Such a total blockage of the sun, of course, would cause a tremendous drop in the earth's temperature, in turn causing surface temperatures to drop below freezing, which in turn would cause plants to die. Scientists refer to this as a "nuclear winter." The herbivores (plant-eating creatures) had a dwindling food supply and began to die rather quickly. The carnivores who prayed on the plant-eaters were thus left without a food source and died shortly thereafter. This obscuring of the sun would have also killed plankton in the oceans, depriving the sea-living dinosaurs of a food source.

By the time the cosmic dust settled and the sun began to shine again, no creatures we would call a "dinosaur" remained alive, although the seeds of plants from that period may well have survived prolonged dormancy and some insects may have survived in egg or pupal stages. Some scientists claim that small mammals also survived, especially those that could burrow or hibernate.

Freezing temperatures would have also caused sources of fresh water to freeze over, which means that many dinosaurs may have died in their search for water. Indeed, most of the remains of dinosaurs seem to be concentrated around what were once river beds or water holes.

In sum, the dinosaurs either starved or froze to death, pretty much *en masse.*

The asteroid that scientists envision was no small fragment from outer space. Scientists believe it was at least ten kilometers (about seven miles) in diameter. Some theorize that its fragments landed near the Yucatan Peninsula, striking the earth with a force equal to 10 million hydrogen bombs! With the explosion, iridium—a platinum alloy—would have been released. Iridium is very rare on earth but common in outer space and there appears to be a marked increase of iridium on earth at the time of the dinosaurs' disappearance.

Other scientists hold to a variation on this theme. They hold that the outer-space mass was actually a comet shower caused by Nemesis, the death star, which they believe orbits close enough to the earth every twenty-seven million years or so, with a gravitational field strong enough to divert comets out of their orbits. The result is that the comets crash into the earth in great numbers, causing the same dust cloud that creates a nuclear winter.

Still other scientists believe the process was started by the eruption of a massive volcano and they point toward the Deccan Traps of India. They believe the increased amounts of iridium could have come from deep within the earth. Again, there's no agreement . . . and nothing provable in a definitive way.

Evolution Science: Concept of Man

What about early man? What about the men and women that may have lived on the earth at the time of the dinosaurs?

Evolution science, in the first place, claims that no men and women were alive at the same time as dinosaurs. Creation science disagrees.

Evolution science further states that man "evolved," and only became man after moving through several species of human-*like* creatures, mostly depicted as apes.

Nearly every person has seen the charts that show an ape progressing ever more upright in stance and ever less hairy to the first "human being" (that still looks remarkably ape-like). Is this a true portrayal of early man?

Let's considered several facts from science and history.

First, many of these "ape-like" drawings that have been created in support of evolution theory were just that: drawings. They were *solely* artist depictions, some of which were drawn from just one bone! In one instance, the *only* remains found on the earth that are attributed to one supposedly transitional figure were two portions of jawbones. How can anyone know what the rest of that creature looked like, much less claim that it was part of man's evolutionary lineage? Talk about the product of imagination .

Second, virtually all of the "apes" in that chart showing the evolutionary progression from ape to man have been shown to NOT be part of a true lineage of man . . . for various scientific reasons. The fact is, most of them were and were finally classified accurately as being ape species.

In one supposedly "prehistoric" man—actually a woman called "Lucy"—the key bone that is supposed to identify this creature as human is a knee joint. The joint itself is not present, however. Scientists have only the upper right leg bone and the lower left leg bone. They have theorized what the joint may have looked like based on opposite leg bones!

In another prehistoric skeleton of man, only a bit of skull has been found. Yet a full drawing of this "early man" has been made showing skin color, hair, and flesh features (including cheeks, nose, and jaw). How can such a full drawing be concocted and then presented as fact based on a bit of skull bone?

The supposed "Java Man?" It has now been shown that "he" was a compilation of a human leg bone and gibbon skull cap. The scientist who put these bones together admitted his error (which had been willful) prior to his death.

The "Peking Man?" This man was conjectured because ape and human bones were found mixed together. Anthropologists now tell us that human beings in that area did, and in some cases still do, consider ape brains to be a delicacy. These human beings may very well have been enjoying a major epicurean treat at the time of their demise. They weren't part ape. They were eating ape!

Early scientists concluded that the swollen joints of "Neanderthal Man" meant that he was in some way not fully formed. More recent theories claim that he may simply have been the victim of the disease we know as rickets.

"Cromagnon Man" was assumed to be primitive because of the primitive nature of drawings found in his cave. Rarely has it been reported, however, that those same cave drawings included human beings in jumpsuits with short sleeves and boots! Not at all primitive.

"Nebraska Man" existed in the evolution science literature for a time. The drawing of this man was based on the discovery of one tooth, which has since been classified as the tooth from an extinct species of pig!

In sum, not **one** credible link has been found to connect monkeys to men. Many scientists are now shying away from this part of the evolution theory, and focusing their studies instead on the ideas of "selection of species."

Third, history simply does not bear out the premise that early man was stupid, clumsy, unspiritual, or lacking in imagination and wit. The exact opposite is what archaeologists have uncovered again and again around the world.

Creation science, by contrast, holds that Adam and Eve were created perfect in every way. They were the most advanced, wise, intelligent, healthy, spiritually sensitive, and fully alive human beings who have ever lived on this earth . . . prior to their sin against God and resulting punishment.

Even as sinful human beings cast out of the Garden of Eden, Adam and Eve continued to be amazing creatures, capable of willful choices and amazing intelligence. They quickly moved from being caretakers to producing crops. They "invented" agriculture—something evolution scientists claim didn't come along for thousands, perhaps millions, of years. They cared for animals in flocks and herds. They studied the heavens and new when the "spring" had officially returned. They had ritual (including the offering of sacrifice to God).

In the first few generations after Adam and Eve, we find the Bible describing people as city builders, musicians, and metal workers. Evolution science would tell us that it took millions of years for man to "evolve" to this state.

Does Archaeology Back up the Bible's Claims?

Again and again, we see evidence of great ancient civilizations. They appeared and disappeared, nearly always after they had entered a very advanced period of nature worship (including worship of heavenly bodies).

Ancient people built cities, using amazing techniques and completing some feats of construction that we are not capable of replicating today! They were capable of moving huge stones across long distances into precise position—something we would have extreme difficulty doing. They built elaborate canal systems. One ancient city unearthed in the Indus Valley had a system of clay pipes for hot and cold running water!

In the artifacts associated with Babylon, archaeologists have found a form of battery, which means that the Babylonians knew about electricity. They have also found electroplated items—artifacts that included aluminum (a metal forged only in very high temperature). One ancient sword has thirteen metals!

Findings around the world tell us that ancient man was a traveler. An inscription has been found in stone on American soil that indicates visitors from Sidon (in the Mediterranean) may have visited the East Coast of America prior to the birth of Christ. The language of Indian people on the East Coast also has hieroglyphics that are remarkably similar to those of the Egyptians.

Ancient people had lavishly decorated jewelry and pottery. They had artistic sense and from the earliest times, had music and musical instruments.

Ancient observatories calculated the days in the year with a math formula carried out to the fifth decimal point.

Archaeologists have found evidence of early surgical and dental procedures. Ancient people developed antibiotics and used optics.

These findings are not limited to one area of the world. Very advanced ancient cities have been found around the world.

Evolution science claims that man is on an upward spiral—that man today can do what man prior to him could not do, and that the pattern of growth has been a steady one from primitive to advanced.

The evidence from archaeology simply does not bear that out.

No Humans Unless Dinosaurs First

Perhaps the most insidious of conclusions drawn by evolution science is that man would not, could not, and did not develop **except** as conditions were made possible by the shift out of the Cretaceous era. The statement is made repeatedly in evolution-science literature that the demise of dinosaurs paved the way for the evolution of man. If conditions had remained such for dinosaurs to have survived, man could not have evolved.

A Political Agenda

What we need to recognize is that evolution science has a political agenda.

The agenda today to **advance** the teaching of evolution science is rooted firmly in a desire to advance a system that denies the existence of God. The strongest advocates of the theory are among the strongest voices denying God's existence, much less His involvement with human beings.

Listen closely to the words and tone of voice used by evolution scientists, evolutionist educators, and evolution science advocates. You will find virtually **no** worshipful references to God the Creator.

8

Dinosaurs and Creation Science

Scientists come in two varieties, for the most part, and certainly in dealing with the subject of dinosaurs.

The evolutionary scientists look at a world they claim is hundreds of millions of years old, and they place dinosaurs in a period of 65–225 million years B.C.

Creation scientists believe that dinosaurs were created by God as a part of the creation described in Genesis 1, and that they were destroyed, for the most part, by Noah's flood.

The biblical creation model is worth exploring in detail since it is a viewpoint held by many—if not most—Bible-believing scientists today.

The biblical model of earth history divides the world into two major periods separated by a catastrophic event:

I

The Early Earth

II

The Great Flood
(complete with earthquakes, volcano
eruptions, and atmospheric calamity)

III

Today's Earth

We'll look at each of these periods along with the major arguments put forth by creation scientists . . . .

Creation Science: The Early Earth

Creation scientists see God as the Source and Originator of all that we know as the universe.

Creation science **states that God is Creator.**

Evolution science claims the process of evolution happens of its own accord, apart from God's involvement. Creation scientists claim by contrast that:

- All of creation is God-initiated and God-governed.
- God created the earth and all living organisms on it.
- Each organism was created to reproduce *after its own kind.*
- Creation was a six-step, or six-day process.
- The earth that existed as the original Creation was quite different than the earth as we know it today.

(See Genesis 1 and 2, Exodus 20:11, and John 1:3.)

Creation scientists and evolution scientists seem to agree on several points:

- *Both agree on the presence of space, matter, and energy in the formation of the earth.* The Bible speaks of the "heavens" (*shamayim*), "earth" (*erets*), and "light" as being the essence of creation. Light, of course, would include the whole electromagnetic spectrum and everything we know today as "energy."
- *Both agree that water is a medium for life.* Evolution scientists, however, see life as arising **from** the water. Creation scientists see God as **using** the waters in His creation. Most of the earth's surface today is covered with water. Most *of* any living creature's chemical composition is water. The earth's atmosphere is a "watery" atmosphere.

- *Both seem to agree that at one time, all of the earth's land mass was unified.* Scientists have given this mass the name Panagea. Creation scientists point toward Genesis 1:9,10—"Then God said, 'Let the waters under the heavens be gathered together into one place, and let the dry land appear;' and it was so. And God called the dry land Earth, and the gathering together of the waters He called Seas." It stands to reason that if the seas are gathered into one place, the land would also be one unified mass.

- *Both agree that at some point in the past, the earth was a lush subtropical paradise, from pole to pole.*

Creation science advocates a subtropical original earth under a "canopy" of water vapor in the upper atmosphere.

Genesis 1:6–7 describes what happened on the second day of creation:

Then God said, "Let there be a firmament in the midst of the waters, and let it divide the waters from the waters." Thus God made the firmament, and divided the waters which were under the firmament from the waters which were above the firmament; and it was so.

From this account, creation scientists speculate that a canopy of water vapor surrounded the earth. The atmosphere was like a "strip of air" between the waters on the earth and this outer water layer.

Such a watery canopy would have had several effects. In the first place, it would have created a "greenhouse effect." The warmth of the sun, as captured by the air cushion between the two water layers, would create a fairly even, warm temperature around the world—a condition both creation and evolutionary scientists agree would be an ideal atmosphere for dinosaurs, as well as other animals and even man.

Indeed, subtropical life forms have been found all over the earth: in northern Canada, on the New Siberian Island (where fruit trees sixty feet tall have been frozen in the ice, along with the trees' fruit!), in northern Alaska (where sloths and saber-toothed tigers normally associated with jungle climates have been found in the ice), and on the Axel Heiberg Islands off Greenland (where fossils of giant redwood trees have been found). Alligator, turtle, snake, and salamander fossils have all been found north of the Arctic Circle.

Creation scientists project that this water canopy—which was actually frozen water (crystalline form)—created a shield that filtered out ultraviolet light and simultaneously, created a greater atmospheric pressure on the earth than we have today.

Creation scientists have calculated that the atmosphere of the Early Earth had an atmospheric pressure of "2," an "air" that was significantly thicker or denser than the air we breathe today.

Such an atmospheric pressure would allow for several phenomenon:

- Small lung capacity in very large creatures (which must have been true for the dinosaurs). Dinosaurs could not have survived on today's "weaker" mixture of air; their lungs would not have been able to absorb enough oxygen.
- Large winged creatures to fly. The *Pteradactyl* could not fly in today's atmosphere—but they could have flown easily in an atmospheric pressure of 2.
- Not only blood cells would be saturated with oxygen, but all plasma.

This last feature means that life forms could have been much greater in size and have lived significantly longer.

The fossil record bears this out, too. For example:

- Cattails today grow to 7–8 feet in height, with about a 12-inch cone. Early earth cattails grew to be sixty feet in height, with a ten-foot cone!

- Dragonflies today have a wingspan of about four inches. Early Earth dragonflies had a wingspan of thirty-six inches!

- Dinosaurs were not the only animals that grew large. Fossils show that a number of animals in ancient times grew larger than their related species today. A beaver fossil has been found that measured eight feet! The earth once had giant kangaroos, deer, and bears.

The Bible speaks in several places of giants roaming the earth. It is very likely that if other species were large in size, human beings were also.

Creation scientists hold, of course, that such an atmospheric pressure can be replicated, and results achieved that should be very similar to what is found in the fossil record if their calculations are correct.

Japanese scientists have done just that. They have grown a tomato plant in a hyperbaric chamber that is now five years old, thirty feet tall, and which yields 5,000 tomatoes!

In a natural hyperbaric chamber, one of the tribes that lives in the Andes dwells at 6,000 feet, in the midst of 11,000 foot mountains. Normally, such an altitude would make for oxygen-poor blood. The people live under a constant cloud cover, however, that creates a different atmospheric pressure. Many of the people there are more than 100 years old, and are still doing heavy physical work!

Creation Science: The Diversity of Species

Creation scientists and evolution scientists clash dramatically when it comes to the origin and diversity of living creatures.

Evolution scientists point toward vertical evolution (mutation of one species into another) through history. Creation scientists claim that each species was created as a distinct, unique, and purposeful species, with "horizontal" variation occurring over time (selective breeding).

Creation science allows for organisms and species to die, and to become extinct.

With the Fall of man into sin, as told in Genesis 3, death entered creation. With death comes violence, as evidenced by the killing of Abel by his brother Cain. (Genesis 4) Death and violence entered the animal world as well as the human world. Species can—and still do—become extinct through the death process. Extinction, however, is not part of an "evolutionary" process—rather, the death process.

Creation science allows for creatures to exist in varying proportions at different times in history.

With death and violence comes a fallen "distortion" of the original perfect balance in Creation. Evolution hinges on a "survival of the fittest" idea. Creationism allows for survival of the fittest, but within and among species—not to the **replacement** of one species by another species. The strongest creatures within a species did, and still do, survive—and their genetic traits are passed on. We see this in fairly recent history with the breeding of horses—which as recently as 500 years ago, were much smaller than they are today. We also see this in human beings. As medical science and nutrition science have advanced, human beings have been growing taller in the last two hundred years—perhaps as much as an average of one inch per generation in certain areas and in certain populations!

The buffalo once roamed the plains of the Midwest. Death and violence "distorted" their existence. The buffalo, however, were not **replaced** by a new order of **species**, as evolution states. They were simply **reduced** in **number** —with the possibility of becoming extinct.

Creation science **allows for an organism to develop multiple forms within the same species.**

Genetic make-up and cross-breeding, and other factors such as isolation and environmental influences, may have affected (as they still do) adaptations and variations within a species.

Thus, different breeds of dogs exist today that did not exist 200 years ago. But . . . all are **dogs**. Different breeds of roses also exist and are cross-bred into existence every year. But . . . all are **roses**.

There is no biological evidence, however, for one organism to change into a completely different kind of organism (either gradually or in sudden leaps)—and to continue to replicate that mutation. No intermediate life forms have been discovered (that is, organisms showing characteristics of evolving into another more complex kind of organism) either in the geological findings or in the biological world.

Creation science **holds to a position that all God's creatures were made with an ability to produce "after their own kind."**

God's creatures were all made with an ability to reproduce. Plants were of three types, according to the Bible— grasses, herbs, and fruit trees. Each had some type of "seed" that allowed it to reproduce. (See Genesis 1:11-12.)

Repeatedly in the first chapter of Genesis, we find these words, "according to their own kind." (verses 21, 24, 25)

There's nothing about the nature of dinosaur bones that indicate they were of a different "life form." In other words, they were made of the same "dust of the earth" as we know it today. Their life form was similar, although not identical, to other creatures that had bones, bone marrow (and thus, blood and a circulation system), brains, and so forth. Isn't it likely that they, too, reproduced "after their own kind"?

Creation science claims that all species were made in the beginning. Some have died out (become extinct). No new species have "emerged" in history.

Evolution science, by contrast, claims that the oldest period of life had fewer life forms, and that diversity came with evolution. Yet, in Field, British Columbia, scientists have found much richer diversity of species in the older layers, rather than the younger ones. The actual **evidence** resides with the creation science point of view.

Creation Science: Man and All Beasts Together

Evolutionists state that man and dinosaurs are separated by more than sixty million years . . . yet supposedly long extinct "prehistoric" species are being discovered today in remote regions of the earth. Creation science takes a completely different approach.

Creation science claims that man and all creatures— including dinosaurs—coexisted.

The biblical account tells us that Adam was given the authority and ability to "name" *all* of the creatures God had made.

Most creation scientists believe that God created dinosaurs on the sixth day of creation—the day on which God said,

"Let the earth bring forth the living creature according to its kind: cattle and creeping thing and beast of the earth, each according to its kind" and it was so. And God made the beast of the earth according to its kind, cattle according to its kind, and everything that creeps on the earth according to its kind. And God saw that it was good (Genesis 1:24-25). The sixth day, of course, is also the day God made man:

Then God said, *"Let Us make man in Our image, according to Our likeness; let them have dominion over the fish of the sea, over the birds of the air, and over the cattle, over all the earth, and over every creeping thing that creeps on the earth." So God created man in His own image; in the image of God He created him; male and female He created them. Then God blessed them, and God said to them, "Be fruitful and multiply; fill the earth and subdue it; have dominion over the fish of the sea, over the birds of the air, and over every living thing that moves on the earth."* (Genesis 1:26-28)

One of the strongest evidences that man and dinosaurs walked the earth at the same time is found in the stone river bed of the Paluxy River as it flows near Glen Rose, Texas.

In the limestone there, scientists have found what they now call the Taylor Trail—fourteen human prints in a distinct left-right pattern, each print an average of 11.5 inches in length. The most noteworthy feature of this trail is that it is laid down **with** dinosaur tracks, and in a couple of instances, the human footprint intersects with or is "within" a dinosaur print!

Creation scientists also point toward the discovery of an ancient iron hammer. When analyzed, the hammer was determined to be 96.6 percent iron, .74 percent sulfur, and 2.6 chlorine. This formulation is not possible to reproduce in today's environment. The scientists have concluded that this is an artifact from the pre-Noah era.

In addition, a tooth that from all analysis to date appears to be that of a human child, has been found in stone **between** layers of dinosaur fossils. And the fossilized remains of what appear to be a human finger (complete with nail and cuticle ridge) have also been found among dinosaur fossils.

Creation science **holds that man and beast lived together in peace in the Garden of Eden.**

The evolutionary vision of the dinosaur age is one of extreme violence. The world of the dinosaurs is invariably depicted as one governed by the "law of the jungle"—the strong preying upon the weak, sick, or injured . . . the need for food and water incessant . . . herds forming for protection . . . migration necessary to take advantage of food sources.

This view is not shared by creation scientists, who see dinosaurs as coexisting peaceably with other animals prior to the Fall of human beings into sin.

Human beings, creation scientists assert, were created to be vegetarians, or "plant eaters." All animals also were originally vegetarians. (Genesis 1:30) There is no evidence of killing before the Fall. Furthermore, at the time of the Flood, all animals must have been **capable** of living on plants alone since Noah was told to load the ship with every kind of food the animals would need, and animals were not considered part of the food. (Genesis 6:21) "Every green plant" was the sustenance of the Early Earth.

What purpose did dinosaurs play in God's plan for creation? We don't know for sure, and may never find out with certainty. It seems likely, however, that at least one of the functions of dinosaurs was to keep certain types of lush plant life under control—both in height and density. The long-necked dinosaurs could have eaten the foliage of even the tallest trees, and in a thick forest or swamp area, this is important in order for light to reach the ground and give shorter plants an opportunity to grow to maturity.

Dinosaurs moving in herds may have created pathways through the vegetation on earth. They may well have been the original trail blazers.

A number of scientists are beginning to rethink the nature of the dinosaur world. A British geologist, Anna Grayson, was quoted in *The Guardian* newspaper as saying the dinosaur era "was a sort of Garden of Eden type of life . . . with a lot of creatures living together in a fairly settled ecosystem." She believes that even the carnivores were no more violent "than the average lion or vulture; they had to eat to live, but they weren't monsters."

Creation science contends that the nature of the earth changed greatly after man and woman sinned.

When Adam and Eve sinned, however, death came into the world for the first time. With death came violence, as we see when Adam and Eve's son, Cain, killed his younger brother, Abel.

Death and violence also entered the animal world. What started out to be a peaceful coexistence turned into a world filled with violence and death—in such massive proportion that the Bible says God destroyed all life except for the people and creatures taken onto Noah's Ark.

Thorns, thistles, disease-producing viruses and bacteria, blood-sucking parasites all developed as a result of the Fall of man into sin.

It is at this time, according to most creation scientists, that animals began to eat the flesh of other animals. They were not, however, "hunters" as much as they were scavengers, according to creation science.

As scavengers, they were part of the animal and fish species today that eliminate waste and clean up the carnage of dying, rotting flesh.

Once man and woman had sinned and death had entered the world, animals as well as men died. Most, if not all, of these animal deaths may have been natural—that is, from old age, from natural catastrophes such as earthquakes, or from falling rocks and trees. Having certain creatures be scavengers would be highly advantageous for keeping the earth free of rotting, smelly dead animals.

The primary fossil evidence that dinosaurs were hunters comes from a fossil bed in which the bones of several carnivorous dinosaurs were found surrounding the bones of a larger plant-eating dinosaur. There is no way that one can interpret from these bones that the meat-eating dinosaurs *killed* the plant-eating dinosaur . . . only that they were feeding on its flesh.

Creation Science: The Demise of the Dinosaurs

Creation scientists and evolution scientists differ greatly when it comes to the matter of "time."

Evolution science flows from uniformitarianism—which says that time and all natural processes have been uniform from the beginning. Change is gradual.

Creation scientists advocate "catastrophe"—sudden shifts. Change is abrupt and definitive.

Perhaps no place is that difference more clear than in the two approaches to the demise of the dinosaurs.

Creation science advocates the destruction of the
Early Earth by a violent catastrophe.

Creation science holds that flood waters covered the
entire earth, destroying all land animals and human beings except those saved on Noah's Ark. At least one pair of
every air-breathing animal was saved. This Great Flood was
accompanied by volcanic activity, earthquakes, and atmospheric catastrophe. The result was an earth in which land
masses were massively readjusted, and the atmosphere of the
air changed dramatically. (See Genesis 6,7,8; 2 Peter 3:3-7; Psalm 104.)

This flood was a **violent** catastrophe.

Creation scientists hold to the opinion that the Flood
was as described by the Bible—a violent upheaval, followed
by a long deluge of water, and an eroding away of the earth
by water over a relatively short time period, encapsulating
dead species in layers of sedimentary rock that were laid
down fairly quickly.

The Bible account of the flood involves more than
rain, which comes as a surprise to many people. In Genesis
7:11 we read,

*In the six hundredth year of Noah's life, in the second
month, the seventeenth day of the month,on that day all the
fountains of the great deep were broken up, and the windows
of heaven were opened.*

Two things seem to have happened simultaneously.
Eruptions happened from the earth's core, and the heavens began to "open up" and pour down upon the earth.

The fountains of the deep broke.

To what might the "fountains of the great deep" refer?

Many believe these were volcanic explosions and
earthquakes. Volcanic explosions generate vast amounts of

fire, lava, and dust—the dust going miles upon into the atmosphere.

A volcano in Indonesia in 1815 sent dust into the upper atmosphere that created, in the northern parts of the world, extremely cool temperatures. In one newspaper, the year 1816 was called "the year without a summer." Snow fell in New England in June and frosts continued through August. In Europe, crops couldn't grow and thousands of people starved in the resulting famine. **One** volcano created that much dust, to dim that much of the sun's heat. What might numerous volcanic eruptions have done?

Volcanos frequently produce *tsunami*—giant tidal waves. Their power to destroy is widely known.

Earthquakes also sometimes produce fissures that spew water, sand, and lava high into the air. Thunder and lightning can actually flash from explosions within the cracks!

In 1811 and 1912, the Mississippi River Valley was shaken violently by earthquakes. The epicenter of at least one of them seemed to be New Madrid, Missouri. The people there reported:

"The ground shook violently. Giant cracks ran suddenly over the ground like the branches of a tree. Some of the cracks were thirty feet wide and 700 feet long. Water, sand, and something like coal, spouted out of the cracks as high as forty feet into the air.

"The Mississippi River seemed to dry up, leaving boats high on dry land, but suddenly the river water returned in a wall fifteen to twenty feet high, destroying all of the boats along the river banks, drowning forests, and creating new lakes."

(*Dinosaurs and the Bible*, page 20)

After the earthquake, some areas of New Madrid were fifteen feet lower than before.

The windows of heaven opened.

Our concept of the opening of the "windows" of heaven should not be limited to the idea of a strong, unending rain shower.

Evolutionary scientists have long held that the dinosaurs were destroyed when an asteroid, or asteroid shower, or perhaps even a comet shower, hit the earth's surface.

Creation scientists also hold this out as a definite possibility at the time of the flood.

In 1908 a tremendous explosion happened in Siberia. Scientists believe it was caused by a piece of a comet, traveling 130,000 miles per hour, which exploded about six miles above the earth's surface. That explosion knocked down eighty million trees over many miles of forest and killed thousands of reindeer instantaneously!

As in the case of earthquakes and volcanos, such an atmospheric explosion over **water** would cause ocean waves of more than 1,000 feet in height—a tsunami that might go for 600 miles from the point of impact!

The flood was "rain plus!"

Yes, the Great Flood of Noah's time was a violent event! The Bible account gives us ample evidence for imagining it as a time of numerous earthquakes, volcanoes, asteroid or comet hits, and tidal waves—not to mention forty full days of pouring rain. These events were likely all linked together intricately in a catastrophe the magnitude of which we can hardly imagine.

The Bible also tells us that Noah and his family floated on the waters created by the flood for a full year. Meanwhile the earth's surface had changed dramatically. Giant oceans were created by the rushing of waters that came from above and below. Great canyons and rock formations were created. Thousands of feet of mud hardened into layers of rock. Does the fossil record bear this out?

The fossils reveal:

- Billions of organisms buried in thousands of feet of layered mud and sand all over the earth.

- Bones of these creatures are scattered fairly widely, not intact, owing to the violence of the forces that ripped apart land masses, animals, and vegetation. Corpses from natural death, or even those killed by predators, tend to lie fairly intact.

- "Pools" of bones are found clustered together where tidal waves had cast them, or currents had swept them, and then had receded fairly quickly into newly formed oceans and seas.

- Certain layers of rock don't appear to be in the "right order" (according to evolution science). There's a mountain in Canada, for example, that is called Upside Down Mountain. An older layer of rock is on **top** of younger layers, with a coal seam between the two layers indicating a heavy concentration of organic deposit at one point in history.

- Creatures of "unlike habitat" are buried together. In one fossil bed in France, scientists have found fossils of **ocean** animals, **fresh water** amphibians, and **land** animals (from spiders to reptiles) all entombed together in the same rock. How could this have happened without a major catastrophic event that swept together creatures of unlike habitat? A catastrophic and violent combination of volcanic action, earthquakes, and massive flooding is a highly plausible answer.

- The bones of dinosaurs are, in many cases, described as "fresh." This means that they show virtually no decay or exposure to wind prior to being fossilized.

Creation science **claims that the catastrophic flood that destroyed the Early Earth was sudden and brief.**

This opinion is based partly only on the Bible account— which tells us that the rain occurred for forty days and nights, and that the flood waters remained over the face of the earth for some 150 days. (See Genesis 7:12, 17-24. Comparing Genesis 7:11 and 8:14 we see that the "flood event"—from first catastrophic event to dry ground—was just a few days longer than one year.)

The concept of a sudden Flood is also based on science and what it takes for something to become "fossilized."

These are the three necessary ingredients for fossilization:

1. Water, in right proportion to other materials.
2. Suitable materials (the right chemicals).
3. Quick burial. Almost immediate encapsulation is necessary.

Evolution scientists claim that brief very localized catastrophic events created conditions that were right for creatures to be encapsulated. They also claim that it is only over a very long period of time that encapsulated bones become fossils.

Creation scientists disagree on this last point. The fact has been proven repeatedly: all fossils are not millions of years old. Some are not even thousands of years old! When conditions and materials are right, bones can become fossils fairly quickly.

Fossilization can happen quickly.

Scientists have found that both wood and chicken bones, when placed with the right minerals in the right amount of water, can become fossils in just five to ten years!

Even the largest dinosaur bones would only take a few hundred years to completely mineralize if the conditions were right.

Consider this fact, too. Many of the dinosaur bones found today are still partially bone, not stone. They are not fully fossilized, but still have characteristic of bone. When some dinosaur fossils are cut with a diamond saw, for example, the odor of burning bone can be detected. Some of the bones have been analyzed—and specific proteins and amino acids isolated. And consider this—some fish fossils still smell fishy when they are first uncovered!

If dinosaurs truly died 65–225 million years ago, it's likely **all** of the bones would be stone. If they died out only a few thousand years ago, it is likely that they might be preserved but not turned to stone. The latter is what scientists have found. It is in keeping with the creation science time table of history.

Sedimentary layers can form quickly.

When Mount St. Helen's erupted a few years ago, it created a localized catastrophe, the magnitude of which most Americans had never seen. One of the things which scientists noted in the aftermath of this eruption was that sedimentary layers were formed **very quickly.** These layers were in stratas similar to sedimentary stratas around the world—stratas supposedly thought to have taken millions of years to form. At Mount St. Helen's the same pattern was established within a matter of hours.

Scientists have concluded that sudden erosional patterns are nearly identical to slower ones. Sedimentary layers can be created by a fairly quick-moving flow of water. They do not need to be created over millions of years. It is **erosion** that is the process, not time.

Creation science **contends that the Flood that**
destroyed the Early Earth was a world-wide event.

A fact about which evolution and creation science
agrees is this: most fossilized remains are associated with
water. Evolutionary scientists frequently claim that "local"
floods caused the death of various dinosaur species. Indeed, floods, earthquakes, and volcanic eruptions are the
three main ways of encasing living material in such a way
that they can **become** fossilized. Creation scientists take
this one step further and claim that **all** dinosaur species
were destroyed in a world-wide massive flood event that
included earthquakes and volcanic eruptions.

What evidence do we see of massive flooding?

First, sedimentary rocks cover seventy-five percent of
the earth's land surface. What mighty force could lay
down thousands of feet of mud, *all over the earth*? A great
flood.

Second, fish fossils have been found on the highest
mountains of the earth. Evolution scientists have no way
of explaining just how they got there.

Third, fossil finds close to the North Pole (in northern
Canada) reveal that warm-loving plants and animals apparently died together very suddenly.

Fourth, stories and theories of massive floods exist
around the world—in all regions and across all cultures.

Fifth, remains of dinosaur creatures from like species
and "eras" have been found at a variety of elevations
around the world. Creation scientists have a simple explanation for this: as the waters receded, they left behind their
deposits.

Consider the nature of these fossil finds . . . .

Evidence of massive flooding is found in the Love
Bone Bed in Florida. There, 100 species of vertebrates have

been found—including salt-water and fresh-water species buried together, as well as a number of unique species not identified previously. In one place, camels and turtles were found in the same layers.

In another fossil bed, scientists have found the remains of some 300 dinosaurs. They attribute this mass death to flooding, but with this twist. They claim the flood was a local one—very likely a river at floodstage. They have proposed that one dinosaur attempted to cross this river, tripped, and drowned. The next dinosaur then tripped over him and so forth until 300 dinosaurs had drowned—even though dinosaurs normally are thought to have been capable of swimming. Talk about herd instinct run amuck. Is it so terribly difficult for these scientists to admit that it is **equally** possible that a massive flood or tsunami caught the entire herd by surprise?

Scientists are realizing that as they compare records of fossil finds, "local" floods seem to have killed dinosaurs around the world at just about the same time. Is it so difficult to carry that conclusion one step further to talk about a Great Flood, one of universal proportions?

Creation science regards the Flood as an act of God's judgment.

Evolution science, of course, would make no such claim since it does not accommodate the concept of a creator God.

Bible-based creation scientists—those who not only take the creation science approach but believe in the whole of God's Word—not only deal with "what" caused events to happen in the Bible, but "who" They see events in the Bible, and in science and history, as "consequences"—not as "coincidences."

Who caused the flood? Creation science tells us, "God did." Actually, as a minister of the Gospel, I believe that this conclusion is not entirely accurate.

The view stated by the Bible is that **man** caused his own destruction through disobedience to God. God's response to man was judgment, but without man's willful disobedience and sin, God would have had no reason to choose—*as is His choice as the Creator!*—to wipe out His original creation and begin anew.

It's like the child who doesn't study, hardly ever attends class and when he does, doesn't pay attention, earns 40 percent on every test and assignment, and then complains loudly, "The teacher flunked me."

Man "earned" the judgment of the Flood through his sinful response to God—a response of willfully desiring to act separately and independently from God.

That's a sobering thought.

Creation Science: Today's Earth

In a summary overview, creation scientists believe that the atmospheric conditions after the Flood became very different than those prior to the Flood, allowing for a wide variation in climate, and thus, a wide variation in plant life, and thus, a wide variation in animal life. Climate variations also caused herding instincts as groups of animals sought to move together in safety to warmer, or cooler, climates—and to follow replenished vegetation. Man, too, became nomadic—wandering after the herds in order to feed himself and until he found areas that were conducive to farming. (See Genesis 8,9,11; Job 37,38; Psalm 104.)

Creation science **believe that dinosaurs survived the Flood.**

Were dinosaurs on Noah's Ark?

Creation scientists believe that they were. They point out that if man and dinosaur did exist at the same time, Noah would have been compelled to take two of every kind of animal onto the ark—including dinosaurs.

Could the ark have supported massive dinosaurs? Yes, in infantile or "egg" form! The "chicks" of even the giant *sauropods* (such as *Brachiosaurs*) are only 12–18 inches long at birth. Some people have even conjectured that all of the animals taken on board the ark were in baby form, for easier care, minimum food, easier loading of the boat, and maximum use of space. The ark may well have been a floating zoo nursery!

One thing creation scientists agree upon is the fact that the earth and the atmosphere surrounding it was different after the Great Flood.

Creation science* believes the earth AFTER the Great Flood was very different.

Noah was no doubt in for a major shock when he and his family stepped off the ark. He and his family had left a lush subtropical environment in which all the land was gathered together, surrounded by seas that seemed to have no end.

He stepped off the ark into a world in which **most** of the land was still covered by water—a fact that continues to this day. Seventy percent of the earth's surface is still water.

All of the familiar landmarks would have been gone. Mud and rock would have been everywhere. Foliage would just have started to regrow and "re-green" the planet. The atmosphere was much drier and the sun would have felt much hotter and more direct. Overall, however, the world would have been a much cooler place. In Job 37:8–10 we see mention of this:

126

The beasts go into dens,
And remain in their lairs.
From the chamber of the south comes the whirlwind,
And cold from the scattering winds of the north.
By the breath of God ice is given,
And the broad waters are frozen.

Is this a mention of the ice age that may well have followed the Flood? Very possibly.

Even a slightly cooler earth would have resulted in millions of species of plants no longer existing, and with the elimination of plants, the elimination of the animals that fed upon them. Large glaciers could have made it impossible for certain species to continue to exist.

Creation science holds that God altered the relationship between man and beast after the Great Flood.

After the Great Flood, God gave Noah and his family permission to kill animals for food and to eat them. Initially, man had not been authorized to eat both plants and meat. (See Genesis 9:2,3.) Now, he was allowed.

Noah and his family could even have eaten dinosaurs, assuming that they tasted good to them. It was not until a long time later that God instructed His people to avoid eating certain flesh, and then primarily for disease-avoiding purposes. The animals and practices considered "unclean" in the Bible have all been proven to be practices advantageous for avoiding food-poisoning, unhealthful bacteria, and foods that might readily lead to disease in human beings.

This permission to "kill and eat" also means that a significant change was made between the way mankind and animals regarded one another. Genesis 9:2 gives us these words of the Lord to Noah, "And the fear of you and the dread of you shall be on every beast of the earth, on every bird of the air, on all that move on the earth, and on all the fish of the sea. They are given into your hand."

The implication, of course, is that mankind and the beasts were not afraid of each other prior to the Flood, and that they coinhabited the earth in peace. (This same pattern of animals and man living together in peace, by the way, is a concept that is also reserved for the Future Earth—the creative order that will be put into place once the Messiah rules the earth and His peace is established throughout creation). (See Isaiah 11:6-9.)

What about God's rules for the animals? They were explicitly forbidden by God to kill people. Genesis 9:5 has these words of God to Noah: "Surely for your lifeblood I will demand a reckoning; from the hand of every beast I will require it, and from the hand of man."

The Bible does not say, however, that animals were forbidden to kill other animals for food in the world after the Flood.

The need for scavenging animals would have been particularly great after a catastrophe such as the Flood. Until the forests and foliage regrew into a lush state, and with no doubt billions of dead creatures unburied on the earth's surface, the eating of animal carnage would have been very likely.

God's rules regarding the eating of flesh make a great deal of sense after the Great Flood. The earth would have been depleted of many of its vitamins and protein with the loss of plant life. Animals may very well have been needed to fill these food "gaps" for the human beings who had lived in the ark.

This change in the relationship between men and animals, and between animals themselves, may have contributed greatly to the disappearance of the dinosaurs.

In sum, there are three possible ways supported by the Bible and creation science for their demise.

1. After the Great Flood, the nature of the earth and the change in the earth's atmosphere, may not have been conducive for them to live. Indeed, their "purpose" for living may have disappeared. The earth was no longer a lush subtropical world that needed their continual harvesting, foraging, and scavenging.

2. After the Great Flood, man was given permission to hunt for food, and the few dinosaurs that began to repopulate the earth after the flood may have eventually been hunted into extinction.

3. After the Great Flood, the natural course of interaction among the species may very well have caused dinosaurs to become extinct, just as species continue to become extinct in our world today (with and without intervention by man). In the last 350 years alone, almost 400 known species have disappeared.

Creation science holds that the change in the earth included these specific differences:

- *The change in the earth's atmosphere resulted in much smaller plants and animals, for the most part.* This is born out in the fossil record and by observation of plant and animal life today.

- *a dispersal pattern of humans from a central point on the earth.* This is born out in archaeological sites as well as legends and myths.

- *a warm ocean (after the superhot volcanic activity associated with the Great Flood).* A warm ocean allows for shifting wind and water currents that would create a rapid and short post-Flood Ice Age arising around the north pole. This is born out in the geological evidence.

- an *earth in which land formations might continue to shift, but without a major flood.* God's promise to Noah was that He would never again destroy "all flesh" by a flood. (Genesis 9:15) Our earth today continues to experience earthquakes, volcano eruptions, and local floods, but with the "canopy of water" above the earth removed, the capacity for a world-wide flood is gone.

Might Dinosaurs Still Be Alive?

If dinosaurs survived the Great Flood on Noah's Ark, evolution scientists argue that there should be some evidence of that.

Creation scientists respond, "There has been and is!"

Not all creatures died during the shifts from period to period. Ammonites, once thought to be alive only in the Cretaceous period are now found in layers of sediment described as Triassic—millions and millions of years apart, according to evolution science.

Others claim that dinosaurs have been and still are being sited in our modern age.

Do *Pterosaurs* Still Fly?

What about *Pterosaurs*? They supposedly died out sixty-five million years ago.

Yet in 1856, railway workers in France were digging a tunnel. They blasted an area with gunpowder to remove a boulder, and when the dust settled, the workmen found a huge bat-like creature. It was stunned, but not dead. The workers brought it out into the light and it began to shake its wings, made a horse cry, and died shortly thereafter.

The creature had a long neck, rows of sharp teeth in a long beak-like mouth, and was shiny black. It's wingspan measured more than ten feet! A scientist concluded that it was, indeed, a *Pterosaur.*

Pterosaurs are not supposed to have lived anytime close to the era of man, according to evolutionary scientists. In fact, they are supposed to be tens of millions of years apart! One apparently survived until 1856.

Do *Plesiosaurs* Still Swim in the Oceans?

What happened to the great sea dinosaurs? An old Hebrew legend says that only three animals survived the flood besides those on the ark. They were the "giant og, the monster reem and the fishes." The word "og" means gigantic and long-necked. *Plesiosaurs*?

Plesiosaurs, the giant dinosaurs of the ocean, disappeared millions of years ago, according to evolutionary scientists.

Yet . . .

On April 10, 1977, a Japanese fishing boat pulled in an unexpected catch off the coast of New Zealand. Their net held the rotting remains of what they regarded as an ocean reptile. The captain tossed the carcass back into the sea, but took photographs and made measurements first.

The creature was thirty-two feet long and weighed about 4,000 pounds. It's skin was pinkish-red in color. Photographs show a long neck and fins on an otherwise reptile-like creature.

The Japanese fishermen took a sample of the creature's flesh back to Japan and a scientist at the National Science Museum concluded it was a *Plesiosaur*! Furthermore, the scientist deduced that the animals are not only **not** extinct, but that there must be a group of them still surviving in the ocean depths since these creatures could not survive more than sixty million years **alone.**

European and American scientists dismissed the finding, but it was called the "scientific discovery of the year" in Japan, and the country even issued a postage stamp to honor the discovery.

And . . .

A few years ago, the U.S.S. Stein tangled with an unknown creature on its way to track submarines near South

America. The ship returned to the Long Beach Naval Dock-yard when its sonar went out. The ship was put in dry dock and when the crew examined the underwater sonar dome, they found the rubber cover that normally protects the dome torn and tattered with dozens of large gouges. Hundreds of sharp hollow teeth (or possibly claws) were still in the rubber—some of these were longer than an inch. To date, scientists have not been able to associate these teeth or claws with any known species.

Do *Coelacanth* Still Swim?

Consider, too, the *Coelacanth*. This is a fossil fish that for decades, scientists believed became extinct some sixty million years ago. In fact, they used this fish as a part of their "index fossil" system. In other words, any rocks that had coelacanth fossils in them were assumed to be sixty million years old, and all other fossils in those rocks were thus considered to be at least that old, too.

In 1938, however, a fishing trawler brought in a catch and as the fishermen were sorting through their catch on the dock, they found a fish they had never seen before. It was nearly six feet long, had powerful jaws, heavy rough scales, and strong lobe-shaped fins. It was steel blue with pink blotches. The fish was taken to a university laboratory. Without a doubt, it was a *Coelacanth*!

Other living *Coelacanth* have been found since then and photographs have been taken of them as they cruise near the ocean floor.

Yet until 1938, scientists believed that mankind and *coelacanths* could not possibly have existed at the same time.

Is Leviathan Still Around?

Leviathan may very well have been a *Kronosaurus*. This was a large reptile with great, sharp teeth, fast-swimming, with strong jaws and protection on its back and undersides. Psalm 104 describes them as swimming where the ships travel, probably the Mediterranean. While not a true dinosaur, this was a very large reptile, a close cousin to the dinosaur, and a creature we do not see in today's oceans (at least as far as we know to date).

One may have been spotted in 1915 in the North Atlantic. The British steamer *Iberia* was torpedoed by a German submarine and sank quickly. A few seconds after the steamer went down, a violent explosion broke the water and pieces of wreckage shot out of the sea. Along with the wreckage came a gigantic sea animal, writhing wildly. It was seen by the German submarine captain, his offers on watch, the chief engineer, the navigator, and the helmsman. None of them had ever seen a creature like it before. They described it as being about sixty feet long, crocodile in shape, with four limbs, webbed feet, and a tail that tapered to a point.

Are There Any *Sauropod's* Roaming the Jungles?

In recent years, American and Japanese scientists have been searching the jungles of Africa for a dinosaur the natives call Mokele-Mbembe!

Large animals have been reported in the swamps of the "Congo" area for decades. One native said that in 1980, he saw a reddish-brown animal rise from the water in front of his canoe. The creature had a "snake-like head" six to eight feet long. As he paddled away, he saw the animal's back appear. In looking at photos offered by missionaries, he identified the animals as a *Ssauropod*, a plant-eating dinosaur.

Another native, a young girl, was paddling her canoe along the shore of Lake Tele when her boat became stuck on a sand bar. As she tried to dislodge her boat, suddenly a large animal broke the water's surface with a great deal of splashing. The frightened girl could not tell the animal's head from its tail, but she did see it's body. She described it as being the size of four elephants. Her parents found her in shock and crying for help. They went to the place where she had apparently seen this mysterious creature and found large, unrecognized foot prints for hundreds of feet along the lake shore.

Have We Really Discovered
ALL of the Earth's Species?

Scientists believe there may be as many as several thousand plant, animal, and insect species that have yet to be "discovered" on the earth and classified.

Perhaps one of them is the "kongamonto?" Native people in northern Zimbabwe have described a flying animal they call "kongamonto." They say it is not a bird, but more like a reddish-colored lizard with bat-like wings (and no feathers). Reports of its wingspan vary from four to seven feet. When shown a picture of a Pterodactyl, the people responded, "Kongamonto!" The creatures supposedly live in a very dense area called the Jiunda Swamp. This area, by the way, is very similar to the descriptions evolution scientists and creation scientists agree would have been typical of the subtropical Early Earth.

And what about . . .

The Loch Ness monster? Big Foot?

Other mystery creatures about which we hear tales, but have few sightings?

They may very well be creatures remaining from another age . . . ones thought long extinct or as never having coexisted with mankind!

Creation Science and Earth's Timetable

As mentioned previously, evolution scientists hold to the opinion that life on the earth existed billions of years ago (estimates vary widely but most put the figure somewhere in the 4–6 billion year range).

Creation scientists point to several interesting facts and ideas in support of this position:

First, scientists are recognizing in increasing numbers that the magnetic field of the earth is being reduced by half every 1400 years. In other words, the magnetic field surrounding the earth was twice as strong in the year 594 as it is in the year 1994. If this pattern of reduction is anyplace close to being constant over time, the magnetic field would have been way too strong to support life beyond several thousand years in history.

Second, scientists had expected the astronauts who landed on the moon to have landed in "deep dust." They had estimated that as much as fifty-four inches of dust covered the surface of the moon—cosmic dust accumulated over the billions of years the moon has supposedly existed. Instead, when the astronauts landed they found only 3/4 of an inch to three inches of dust! The evidence simply wasn't there to support billions of years of accumulation of cosmic debris.

Third, scientists have been able to measure a decrease in the size of the sun over the years. They claim that the sun "billions" of years ago would have been so large that the earth would have been boiling.

Fourth, creation scientists point to a number of facts that seem to indicate the earth's crust is only 5,000–10,000 years old:

- Erosional patterns in the Southwestern United States
- The Mississippi Plain
- The oldest living trees estimated at 5,000 years old
- The life span of Niagara Falls

Fifth, present populations of humans and animals are consistent with models that show a "start" from very small reproducing groups less than 10,000 years ago.

Sixth, while it is not a point made by creation scientists, it *is* the spiritual conclusion of many Christians today (and a growing number of nonbelievers) that mankind, worldwide, has an intuitive, inner sense that things are "winding down."

For centuries, Bible experts have pointed toward the seventh millennium as being "the age of the Messiah." We are nearing that time in recorded calendar keeping.

9

Other Bible-Based Approaches

Apart from creation scientists, there are those who hold other theories about the origin of the universe, and who see a "different design" in the Book of Genesis, or a different role for dinosaurs.

Five of these ideas are summarized below—very briefly, I hasten to add!

1. **God's Method was Evolution.** God "created" the evolutionary process and is the cause behind all apparent evolutionary changes in species. God is Creator. Evolution may have been His method. Dinosaurs, thus, may have existed exactly as evolution scientists claim.

2. **The Bible is a "Spiritual" Book, Not a Science Book.** Scripture relates to the "heart" of man and for the most part, the Bible isn't applicable to science. (In recent years, with so many scientific studies conducted and reported that *support* Bible statements, those who take this approach seem to be modifying their position to take this stance: the Bible is a "spiritual book" that attempts to deal primarily with spiritual matters. It reveals an understanding of the natural world that, to the extent in which it was "revealed by God," is accurate. Nonetheless, an understanding of the natural world is never as *important* an understanding of the spiritual world. Natural matters are important only as they relate to or

impact spiritual concerns.) Dinosaurs are regarded as having nothing to do with a man's soul and are therefore unimportant, and thus, unrecorded in Scripture.

3. **God's Creativity and Purposes are a Mystery.** God created heaven and earth, and we are still learning exactly how He did so—and whether the period described in the first chapter of Genesis should be taken as seven literal days or as even ways—God alone knows. Nonetheless, God is Creator and the general sequence of His creation is as stated in Genesis. Dinosaurs had a place and purpose, although we may never know it.

4. **The Bible Is Only for "This Present Age."** The Bible refers only to our "present age." The opening chapter of the Genesis tells man's understanding about the ancient past, but the remainder of the Bible deals with the era in which we live. Dinosaurs may have been part of a previous era—perhaps, some say, even part of the earth when it was Lucifer's private garden—but they are not mentioned in the Bible because they do not pertain to the history that began with Adam and Eve.

5. **Dinosaurs are Part of God's Secret.** Dinosaurs are simply a part of God's mystery. He hasn't revealed to us their place, purpose, or importance to us.

Variations on these themes have been proposed, of course, and certain positions have been blended together from time to time. It is perhaps important to note that "creation science"—as an organized set of hypotheses with research to support them—is only a few decades old. (Creationism, by comparison, has been an opinion as old as recorded time.)

For a number of years, the primary approach to creation was . . .

The Long-Day Approach

This approach to the story of The Creation in Genesis assumes that God's days may very well have been longer than our days. Those who hold this approach believe that we are incapable of knowing just how "long" a day in creation was . . . that it may have been as the psalmist stated, *For a thousand years in Your sight are like yesterday when it is past* (Psalm 90:4).

They regard The Creation as being a series of seven steps, each with a beginning and ending that was according to God's timetable.

An interesting variation to this approach has been taken by Gerald L. Schroeder in his book, *Genesis and the Big Bang.*

Schroeder, who is both a physicist and a theologian, has a doctorate from the Massachusetts Institute of Technology. He has a world-wide reputation as a scientist, who attempts to bridge the scientific world with the Old Testament. Schroeder believes that "the opening chapters of the book of Genesis and the findings of modern science are in harmony, not in dispute.

Genesis and the Big Bang presents a number of interesting concepts, among which are these four (which are paraphrased here in very simple terms compared to the lengthy mathematically-based discussion in the book):

1. God operated according to a unique time reference in The Creation. Schroeder sees this difference in time as *qualitative*, rather than quantitative. "It has the feel of time *seeming* to pass at different rates for different participants in an event, but not necessarily being different in reality." (*Genesis and the Big Bang,* page 34)

2. In applying Einstein's theory of relativity to the history of the Earth as we know it, Schroeder has come up with a time span of 5.6 days! Genesis records 6 days.

3. Schroeder believes each step of the Creation involves a state of life that "was a unified order." He has calculated that dinosaurs were the unified order that belong to the fifth "day" of creation in which great sea creatures, fish, and birds were made. (Creation scientists place their appearance on the sixth day.)

4. Adam was a distinct *type* of human being, and together with his wife Eve, he is the founder of the specific strain of humanity that exists today—a humanity complete with a spiritual component intended to reflect the image or "shadow" of God on the earth. Thus, Adam and Eve were the first human beings to have a "soul of life."

He makes one point with which certainly all scientists must agree: during the first five days of creation (prior to the creation of man), God alone was watching the clock!

We simply do not know what happened prior to man's creation, and can never know with certainty. God alone holds that knowledge.

What Can We Conclude?

What we can conclude, and what virtually all Jewish and Christian scientists who are creationists believe, is that the Bible is a spiritual book that is God's revelation to us about Who He is and Who we are. The summary statement about that is simple:

God is the Creator.

All else is created, including us.

We are creature. We are finite. We have a beginning and an ending. We were made.

God is Creator. He is infinite. He has no beginning and no ending. He simply is. He is **I am who I am.** (Exodus 3:14)

The order in which God created things, the way He did so, and over what period of time are mysteries for which God alone has **all** the answers at present.

More specifically, Bible-believing people and creationists seem to agree on these two points:

First, *God created the world with an intricate design and such complexity that after thousands of years, we are only now unlocking some of God's "secret ways."*

The mysteries of God are not mysteries **to** God. He knows the beginning from the ending of everything. He knows the fullness of His creation, including the blueprint of every creature now extinct. Just because man hasn't yet "proven" something about God's creation doesn't mean that it wasn't so, or that it didn't exist.

Second, *God hates sin. He is just, and as a part of being just, He must judge sin.*

When man sins, he is not the only one affected. No person can "sin in isolation." Man's behavior determines the fate of other human beings, as well as the fate of plants and animals.

Man's original role was to subdue, replenish, and have dominion over plants and animals. Mankind was designated to be the steward over the rest of creation. When we fail to honor God's creation, we fail in our relationship with God. Not only are we subject to punishment, but the living creatures and plants of the earth suffer.

The present world is described by the Apostle Paul as one that is "groaning" and "in pain," awaiting man's redemption. (See Romans 8:22.) From cover to cover, the Bible presents a picture of man's sin resulting in judgment and sorrow, and man's repentance resulting in deliverance and joy. Man's sin effects everything around him. No person can sin "independently" so that his or her sin has no impact on the lives of others or the environment in which the person lives. Sin has consequences beyond any one person's life.

10

Dinosaurs at the Video Store: Vastly Different Messages

The widely divergent approaches to the origin and development of species—as presented in the previous chapters on Evolution Science and Creation Science—give us a backdrop against which to evaluate the videos about dinosaurs and dragons that line the video store shelves today.

The selection available is highly diverse and not only varies from store to store, but from year to year. Look for key principles in the reviews of the videos in this chapter. They will likely apply to the videos of the future, as well as the other titles in the store from which you rent.

Ancient Dinosaurs and Modern People

Prehysteria (1993) might have been called "Home Alone with Dinosaurs." The plot focuses on frozen dinosaur eggs that hatch and produce baby dinosaurs that basically run wild and create all kinds of slapstick havoc.

The film was made directly on video and rushed into stores just in time for *Jurassic Park's* opening as something of a "piggy back" movie. The dinosaurs are far more cuddly than beastly. They are pet-sized, about the size of cats or small dogs.

The story line is this: A ruthless museum gift shop owner steals some eggs from a secret South American temple—eggs which accidentally fall into the hands of a young boy and his family. The family dog hatches the eggs and at first, the boy and his older sister try to keep their amazing pets a secret from their father, fearful that dad will return them to the gift shop owner. It's hard, however, to keep five dinosaurs a secret for very long.

The creatures are named after rock stars: the *T-rex* is Elvis (the "king of rock" is linked to the king of the dinosaurs), the *Pteranodon* is named Madonna, the *Chasmosaurus* is called Hammer, the *Stegosaurus* is named Jagger, and the *Brachiosaurus* is called Paula.

One of the animators for the movie made an interesting comment, "As you get into your work, you get less interested in photographic reality and more interested in something expressive. The object isn't to be exactly like nature, but to say something more." (*Cinefantastique*, August 1993, page 31)

It's the "something more," of course, that is the concern. What is it that the film-maker really wants to **say**, using dinosaurs strictly as a vehicle for pricking interest and keeping the action flowing?

This is a basic question to ask yourself repeatedly as you preview videos for your children:

What more *is* it the film maker is saying?

In all, the movie was designed more for children than *Jurassic Park*, but I can't fully recommend it—not because of the dinosaur message, but because of the language that occurs periodically in the movie.

Land Before Time is another Lucas and Spielberg collaboration. A popular movie in theaters in the 1980's, it's still a popular video.

The story is that of Little Foot, a *Brachiosaurus*, who joins together with four other dinosaur friends: Petrie (of the "fliers" —a *Pteradon*), Cera (short for *Triceratops*, called in the video "the three horns"), Duckie (one of the "wide mouths," or duckbill dinosaur species), and Spike (a "spike tail" or *Stegosaurus*). All are orphaned temporarily in a series of earthquakes and volcanic eruptions that turns their world upside down and separates them from their families.

At times scared and unsure of themselves, the little dinosaurs nonetheless continue on their migratory trek to the Great Valley, a place they envision to have plenty of food and water. The place they are leaving is a hot desert without food. In the course of their journey, Little Foot's mother dies, the little dinosaurs have several fierce encounters with a *Tyrannosaurus rex*, and they themselves barely escape earthquakes and volcanic eruptions.

The movie presents the straight evolutionary line, with a little addition of Zen philosophy about the "great circle of life" and the importance of "letting your heart guide you" on life's journey. The movie portrays necromancy—communication with the dead, as Little Foot receives encouragement and guidance from his deceased mother.

In the end, the little dinos find the Great Valley and meet up with long lost relatives—in the case of Little Foot, his grandparents.

The cuteness of the movie and the excellence of the animation notwithstanding, this is a movie with a decidedly ungodly message: natural forces govern life, not God. In my opinion, the movie also has a very cheap definition of the eternal value of love.

Denver—The Last Dinosaur is an animated action-hero-style series designed for Saturday morning and after-

145

school audiences. Videos of the series have been released, with two episodes per cassette.

Denver is a cute, green, friendly-faced, ridge-backed, heavy-bottom, pointy-tailed dinosaur that wears pink sunglasses and lives in southern California.

He is a friend of four teens who include him readily in their activities. The bad guys in the series are always foiled without violence.

Denver speaks gibberish, for the most part, but is understood by all the teens. He acts like a big, fun-loving, mischievous, kind-hearted kid. Children will respond to Denver much more than teens, even though Denver is portrayed as a friend of teens.

Baby—Secret of the Lost Legend (Touchstone Pictures—Walt Disney) is a take-off on the African native alleged sightings of "Mokele-Mbembe," which from all accounts sounds like a *Brontosaurus*. In this movie, a young paleozoologist named Susan (Sean Young) and her journalist husband, George (William Katt) are about to complete Susan's six-month post-doctoral research fellowship in Africa when she unearths a *Brontosaurus* vertebrae and then follows a Red Cross doctor to a remote village where a man is dying from food poisoning. In the course of Susan's conversation with the dying man, he draws an outline of the creature he and his dying and sick villagers had eaten—a *Brontosaurus.* This sets Susan and George on a hunt of the area. After an encounter with an African tribe, they do make the find of the century: a *Brontosaurus* family complete with a "hatchling" about the size of a large St. Bernard dog.

Meanwhile the evil Dr. Erik Kiviat (played by Patrick McGoohan) and his assistant Nigel (Julian Fellowes) pursue Susan's bone find, and later are in hot pursuit of the same *Brontosaurus* family that Susan and George have found. Kiviat manages to snare the female *Brontosaurus* and lure the baby into his cage, after killing the male dinosaur.

The movie ends with the mother and baby *Brontosaurus* being reunited with assistance from Susan and George.

The movie has a PG rating, which, in my opinion, is inappropriate. This movie is **not** for children, even with parental guidance! It opens with a stabbing murder and includes another point-blank murder near the end of the movie. It depicts arson, a human body on fire, the grim electrocution of Nigel, a brief war in which natives express joy at killing other human beings, and finally, the bloody killing of Dr. Kiviat by the female *Brontosaurus*. The movie also has several scenes with sexual overtones and a reference to "drug use in college" that I find inappropriate for children. The movie has nudity of the native women and children, as well.

Apart from those features of the movie, *Baby* is a mixed bag of folklore and science. It depicts the scientific world as one of violence and intense jealousy. Susan and George decide to keep their find a part of the "legend" so the dinosaurs might continue to live in peace. (That is hardly realistic given the importance of such a find!) Overall, the movie stands in contrast to a theory that states all dinosaurs died out more than sixty million years ago.

And Then There Are the Dragon Videos . . .

Puff the Magic Dragon (1978, The My Company, distributed as part of the Children's Video Library) is a short animation of the song that Peter Yarrow and Leonard Lipton made popular in the 1960's. The video tells how Puff—a green stringy-haired, bow-tied, curmudgeony dragon that blows pink puffs—comes to little Jackie Draper, a sorely depressed and withdrawn boy. Jackie, in the opinion of medical experts "can't speak, relate, or communicate" with the world—a fact obvious to his parents —and the only hope for him lies in a "miracle," which the medical experts soundly state is not what they expect. Puff takes the child's "soul" out of him and puts it onto a paper cutout, which becomes an animated "boy." He builds a boat with this boy and together, they travel to Honalee. As they journey, they encounter a big mean pirate who becomes a baker. Upon their arrival at Honalee, they find that the island isn't at all the way Puff remembers it or Jackie imagined it to be. It has been overtaken by "living sneezes"—which are cured when the once-pirate, now Baker shows up with a big pot of chicken soup.

On the journey to Honalee and back, Jackie overcomes his fears about the sea, about big people, and about life in general, and in so doing, overcomes his depression and begins to speak. Puff is then free to depart and move on to other children in need.

The video presents Puff as a friendly rascal. The story line has no violence and no truly frightening moments, but in all, the tale is a bit absurd and likely to be difficult for young children to follow.

The message, however, is one that is very much rooted in today's "Zen"-based New-Age thinking—and that is the message that one's salvation lies within. If a person can simply overcome his or her fears and take an inner voyage, of sorts, in order to confront life and develop courage . . . then one can emerge whole and healthy and capable of relating to and loving others. Christianity, by comparison, takes the approach that it is the Holy Spirit who brings about a person's regenerated mind and heart, and that the Holy Spirit enters into a person's life only upon one's acceptance of

Him, through belief in the Lord Jesus Christ and an act of receiving the Spirit.

Puff is regarded as a vehicle for releasing Jackie's fears. In some ways, he is Jackie's "spiritual guide." Let's not lose sight that this so-called "folk song" and its message came out of the 1960's, a decade in which drugs and the smoking of marijuana were regarded as a means of releasing a person's inhibitions and fears, and of opening a person up to a broader and more beautiful reality, one in which they were capable of "free love" to all people. All of the elements of that era and its underlying philosophy can be seen in this video, although as mentioned previously, the young viewer isn't likely to understand that message clearly or directly from the visuals and dialog.

Serendipity—The Pink Dragon (1989, Fuji Eight Co., Inc.) is a full-length animated feature. The introductory song actually identifies Serendipity as a *dinosaur*, and since she is quite friendly, has no scales or legs, never displays the abilities of breathing fire or flying, and actually looks much more like a cross between a *Brachiosaurus* and a *Plesiosaur* . . . we should probably consider Serendipity to be a dinosaur and not a dragon.

The story is that of Bobby who travels to Antarctica with his marine biologist parents and becomes separated from them when the area in which he is playing breaks off the mainland and becomes an iceberg.

Bobby rides the melting iceberg—which melts to the point of being a "big pink orb"—to a South Sea island named "Paradise." The orb, of course, is an egg, and when it hatches, out comes Serendipity. She is pink, with huge blue eyes and a green ridge of plates along her back. She has a longish tale and two fins (which amazingly allow her to swim and climb mountains with equal ease). Her voice is that of a kind little girl.

Paradise is ruled by a kindly Princess Laura, who is advised by a bespeckled wise dolphin named Lord Winston.

"Aquanuts" serve Princess Laura. Shaped rather like big green water droplets with legs, they cry on Princess Laura's behalf, and convey her messages to the inhabitants of the island. Professor Abraham is the wisest creature on the island, which is guarded by a loyal and kind military regiment of sharks.

Once Serendipity and Bobby arrive in Paradise, they meet up with Pela-Pela, a talkative and rebellious female parrot (whom Bobby had first met on the steamer that took his family to Antarctica). Pela-Pela continually gets in trouble and actually causes a major threat to the island, but is lovable nonetheless.

All in all, Paradise is paradise. Captain Smudge makes several attempts to find the island (desiring to exploit its gold). Bobby leads the others in thwarting his attempts.

The video presents the relationship between mankind and dinosaurs as a kindly, mutually supportive one. There is no violence or killing. The pace is slow enough and the story clear enough for young viewers to enjoy the tale. Perhaps the most troubling aspect of the video is the separation of the boy Bobby from his parents.

One might also argue that Pela-Pela *should* serve the full ten-day sentence as imposed by the judge and jury that finds her guilty of leaving the island without permission. (She is never required to serve the term in the video.)

These are points worth discussing with a child, but are not objections that would keep me from recommending the video as a good story for young viewers.

Pete's Dragon (Walt Disney Productions) is a combination of animation and live action. Elliott, the big green dragon with a shock of pink hair and small pink wings, is animated. He looks like a fat *Stegosaurus* with a plate-like ridge along his back and a long flexible tail (sans spikes). All other characters are real.

Pete (played by Sean Marshall) is an orphan boy who has been "purchased" by a wicked family named Grogan. The Grogans (Shelley Winters plays Ma Grogan) only want to use Pete to do the hard labor on the family farm. Pete escapes with help from Elliott and after a brief escapade in the next town to which they travel, he is befriended by lighthouse keepers Lampie (Mickey Rooney) and his daughter Nora (Helen Reddy). Elliott sleeps in a cave near the lighthouse.

Elliott speaks gibberish that only Pete can understand. Pete is also the only one who can see Elliott when the dragon makes himself invisible. Elliott, meanwhile, has a great propensity for mischief—the punishment for which tends to fall on Pete.

The plot thickens when a dishonest money-hungry snake-oil salesman, Dr. Terminus (played by Jim Dale), comes to town. With his sidekick Hoagy (Red Buttons), Dr. Terminus plots to buy and then steal Elliott for their purposes. As a side plot, Nora awaits the return from the sea of her fiance, hoping against hope for his safety even after news that his ship had broken apart in a storm.

The video is G-rated and has some nice messages. Helen Reddy sings an endearing song to Pete that conveys "it's not easy to find magic in pairs." In the end, Nora's fiance does return, Dr. Terminus and Hoagy are run out of town, the Grogans see their "claim" to Pete go up in Elliottinduced flames, Pete finds a new home at the lighthouse, and Pete goes on to help the next boy in need.

The video has a great deal to do with wishes coming true, and nothing to do with evolution. Children will likely find it a rousing song and dance story. Some parents may have trouble with the message that Elliott can cause unbelievable havoc (especially when he makes himself invisible) without any recompense or punishment, and are likely to disagree with the related and more subtle message that general "mischief" is actually the result of an invisible and benevolent force.

My qualm with this movie has to do with a standard Disney theme: men and women, and boys and girls, can rely on "magic" —this time in the form of a magical dragon named Elliott—to help them through life's difficult circumstances. Magic, of course, comes guised as love, fortuitous circumstances, and benevolent benefactors. Disney videos, as a whole, present a wide assortment of alternatives to God, the Source of all blessings and the only sure ally that any of us have in times of trouble. Beware of this hidden message in Disney films. The stories seem cute. The happily ever after fairy-tale endings are sweet. But the message is nearly always one that has occultic under-pinnings: "you don't need God . . . you just need a little magic."

Lizard-Monster Tales of Woe

It's only one step from "dragon lore" to lizard-monster tales. The foremost lizard-monster tale, of course, is *Godzilla*.

A number of *Godzilla* take-offs have been produced, and are still being produced. Variations on his theme are too numerous to recount. Think monster movie. Think violence. And avoid.

Unfortunately, the "lizard-monster" theme has become a part of a number of other shows that are aimed directly at children. Watch closely for them. As an example, an episode of the Super Mario Brothers *Super Show* portrays the antics of Koop-Zilla, a regular sized dinosaur-like lizard monster that eats a souped up batch of "super sushi" and becomes a major force for destruction, and violence. As in many of the Super Mario Brothers shows, there's lots of name-calling and fighting. This particular episode includes a fire set in a dynamite factory. If dinosaurs are linked to animated action heroes, you can nearly always assume violence. Again . . . avoid!

The recent Super Mario Brothers movie, by the way, has a midget dinosaur named Yoshi. He's probably in the video stores by now. I suggest you leave him there.

Time Travel Videos Often Include Dinosaurs

A number of story lines in the video stores include time travel to the prehistoric past. The main thing to watch for in these movies is what it takes for the modern-day folk to return back to modern times. Frequently, mass destruction, war, or destruction of dinosaur foes is required. Again, the violence factor runs high. Here's just one review of a time-travel video. It was shelved as a "family video" and everything about its packaging makes it look fun for children . . . .

Adventures in Dinosaur City (1992) is an 88-minute story in which three teenagers (two guys and a girl) play with their parents time-machine in the laboratory located next to their home, and are zapped into a real-life version of their favorite TV cartoon show, "Dinosaur City." The plot involves the ongoing rivalry between Tarry Town and Saur City, and has such characters as Rex, Tops, and Mr. Forry. The walking-talking dinosaurs are smart and the prehistoric "cave people" are goofy and stupid. A battle erupts, of course, in which the teens help win the day for the good guys (a mix of dinosaurs and people). And eventually they figure out how to use the remote control device for the computer/television to return to the current century—just in time for Mom and Dad to return home.

The movie has a lot of violence and some frightening scenes, and has absolutely nothing to do with reality—either from an evolutionist or creationist standpoint. Overall, I found the video demeaning to humanity and from a story standpoint, would consider it a waste of time.

Videos that Attempt to Educate Children

Several videos *about* dinosaurs are in the video stores, usually shelved in the family or children's sections. For the most part, they aren't worth renting. Here are three to watch out for:

Dinosaurs, Dinosaurs, Dinosaurs (1987) is something of an overview of the dinosaur world. The video features Gary Owens, who is suffering from a disorder that seems to be turning him into a dinosaur. He sends his colleague Eric Boardman to the Crystal Palace in London to get "healing water" from the ponds there. Along the way, a smattering of highly diverse information is offered to young viewers.

There's a brief museum tour that describes features of the various dinosaurs on display. There's a display of Dinomation animated dinosaurs, a sequence about dinosaurs in movies, a visit to a would-be dinosaur park (with concrete dinosaurs) located between Los Angeles and Palm Springs, a look at the dinosaur statues at the Crystal Palace, and an artistic display of would-be dinosaur skeletons that are actually made from a conglomeration of brightly painted automobile parts.

In the end, Owens turns into a dinosaur—something of evolution in reverse!—and gets a job as part of a museum exhibit about dinosaurs.

The video does present the basic evolution science line—that dinosaurs lived eighty million years ago and that possums, birds, and salamanders survived (and replaced) dinosaurs.

Overall, the video has no focus. It isn't a bad message as much as it's a slow video with a very thin plot line. The references to evolution are very brief and not made with any impact.

Dinosaurs! (1988) is a 30-minute video that stars Fred Savage as a young boy, Phillip, who is facing the challenge of preparing a science project for school. He gets an idea from a rock song about "Mesozoic Time" sung by a group of animated dinosaurs. As he falls asleep, he hears a "voice" that begins to tell him about fossils. The voice gives an overview of evolution, stating that shallow seas dried up 250 million years ago, forcing dinosaurs to develop on *land*.

The movie has some great animation sequences, including Claymation animation, and is well scripted and visually appealing, but the message is straight out of evolution science textbooks.

Reading Rainbow—Digging Up Dinosaurs features LeVar Burton on a tour of Dinosaur National Park in Utah.

In addition to conversations with the paleontologists at work on the rock formations there, the video features a number of book reviews (the *Reading Rainbow* format). Among the books reviewed are:

- *Dinosaur Wrecks*—a book of dinosaur-oriented riddles by Noelle Sterne, with pictures by Victoria Chess.

- *Dinosaurs!* by Michael Emberley, which is primarily a book about how to draw dinosaurs and pronounce their names.
- *If You Are a Hunter of Fossils—* a "poem with pictures" written by Byrd Baylor and illustrated by Peter Parnall.
- *Dinosaur Time* by Peggy Parish, illustrated by Arnold Lobel.
- *Digging Up Dinosaurs* by Aliki, a book about the work that paleontologists do.

For the most part, the books are based on the evolution "science" view of dinosaurs.

The video presents the message: "If your relatives seem reptilian—and some look like they're even over a million—climb up on your family tree and check your dino history."

A Series to Watch Out For—Rather Than to Watch

Many people look to PBS programs for quality viewing, and thus, may be tempted to rent or purchase the four-part dinosaur series produced by the Public Broadcasting Service in 1992. I don't recommend this series in the least. While it has a great deal of factual information about dinosaurs, the information is presented in a straight evolution science way.

In the first program, titled "The Monsters Emerge," the history of dinosaur fossils is covered, and along with it, the origins of evolution theory.

In the episode "Flesh on the Bones," the way in which characteristics are ascribed to bones is described. (The video does give an interesting description of the Alexander Formula, a method by which length of bones and stride length of tracks are compared to creatures of similar bone size and stride today, to determine just how fast dinosaurs may have moved.)

In the episode titled "The Nature of the Beast," we are told about "early experiments that failed" in the evolution column.

In the fourth episode, "The Death of the Dinosaur" is explained as a mass event of some type that happened to mark the end of the Cretaceous period. Evolution scientists believe such events also marked the end of the Triassic and Jurassic periods. The video ends with this statement: "Humankind owes its existence to the extinction of the dinosaurs."

Four Points of Evaluation

In evaluating videos, you will probably want to keep these four questions uppermost in your mind:

1. Does the video present a creation or evolution point of view?
2. How much violence is involved?
3. Does the story make mankind and animals "equals"?
4. What underlying philosophy about the world does the film maker seem to have?

Not all dinosaur movies are bad. At the same time, not all are well made, scientifically accurate, or morally good! The bad ones can be *really* bad!

If you are interested in the reviews of thousands of movies from a biblical perspective, you should get a copy of *The Christian Family Guide to Movies and Videos*. It's put out by Ted Baer, President of the Christian Film and Television Commission. Baer also publishes a monthly magazine with updated movie reviews. You can contact his organization by calling: (800) 899-6684

11

Dinosaurs on TV:
Two Barneys, and a Family to Avoid

In the opening music for the television program that bears his name, Barney is called a "dinosaur sensation." That may be the understatement of the year. Barney is big, both literally and figuratively.

The oversized purple dinosaur has become a pal to millions of children. His show, *Barney and Friends,* is a music-driven program aired on Public Broadcasting Service (PBS). It is watched by eighty percent of the two-to-five-year olds watching television! He receives 10,000 fan letters a week.

"Mom can't see him," of course. He is a product of imagination.

The program features a number of familiar tunes to which new lyrics have been given—tunes such as "Clementine" and "Give the Dog a Bone." The good news is that two Christian fathers produce and direct the Barney music: Bob Singleton and Larry Haron. (They also arranged and produced *Great Songs for God's Kids*, published by Word Music.)

Singleton and Haron approach the Barney music as *all* children's programming should be approached: with the child kept first and foremost in mind.

Barney was created in 1988 by teachers Sheryl Leach and Kathy Parker. They worked with video producer Dennis DeShazer to create Barney for DLM, Inc., a Texas-based distributor (now RCL Enterprises, Inc.).

The original concept was a very simple one: have a stuffed purple dinosaur come to life "in the imagination" and teach very basic morality lessons to toddlers. The motivation was Leach's own restless toddler. She and her husband Jim saw a series of videotapes as a means of entertaining their own child.

What has resulted is a half-billion dollar business. Barney is not only the star of a PBS program and a videotape series, but a line of toys, a radio program, a show at Radio City Music Hall titled "Barney . . . Live at Radio City!," and a recent television special aired on NBC. A feature-length movie is coming out in the simmer of 1995. More than 200 Barney products have been licensed, from lunch pails to blankets. Plans to take Barney "international" are in the works. He appears at nearly thirty charity benefits a year now. In all, it's easy to see why some have called the phenomenom the "Barney Boom."

The PBS program, *Barney and Friends*, incorporates dance and popular children's songs to teach good health, self-esteem, environmental issues, respect for people of other cultures, and appreciation of friends, among other "neighborly" topics.

The shows have six children who interact with Barney—a true ethnic mix. The children sing and do simple choreography that toddlers and young children enjoy mimicking at home. The rhyme and sing-song nature of the songs makes them easy to learn. Children, of course, love to watch their favorite videos over and over and over and over. After just a couple of viewings, most children are able to sing along with most of the songs.

Barney, as a character, is friendly, positive, and enthusiastic about life. "Oh boy, oh boy, oh boy" seems to be his favorite phrase, usually accompanied by a friendly ho-ho laugh. Barney's appeal seems to lie mostly in the fact that he talks to children. He speaks words of caring to them, and in a world of TV violence and high divorce rates, he's comforting.

The pace of the show is slower than what most adults are used to, and perhaps ironically, slower than what many adults think children *like*. It's a pace that young children enjoy and find able to encompass. In many ways, the program is reminiscent of the kindergarten shows of the 1950's, in which strong, moral family values were taught. Children love it. They seem to know the show was created for them. And parents and critics have highly mixed reviews—perhaps in part because the show's producers did not create the program for the critical acclaim. Probably the main reason parents don't like the show is that it is so-o-o-o-o slow, and highly repetitious. Again, however, these are plus factors for very young children.

One of the best ways to evaluate a children's program is to watch children *watch* the program. When children watch *Barney & Friends*, they tend to play along with the show, sing and dance with the characters, and talk back to the TV set. That's the way children's programs should be—they should evoke participation, not wide-eyed, numbed staring.

Among the Barney videos are:

- *Caring is Sharing* portrays how children and adults can share everything from books and toys to chores and play.
- *Our Earth, Our Home* lets children see how items can be recycled, water conserved, and "habitats" created for animals and birds.
- *Alphabet Soup* teaches the ABC's.
- *Be a Friend* prompts children to reach out to others, make new friends, and introduce friends to others.
- *Playing it Safe* covers traffic lights, seat belts, and what to say to strangers.

The videos are recommended for ages 2-8, but they are geared more for the two-year-old than the eight-year-old.

The April 1994 television special on NBC, titled "Imagination Island" told the story of a toy-making professor with a wonderful imagination who became stranded on an island. Although a genius at making toys, the professor wouldn't share those toys with others. He was a very unhappy man, and couldn't understand why the children were happy. The children teach him to share and together, they devise a way of getting off the island. Barney, as a character, is simply omnipresent, always there and stating the occasional obvious morality lesson, such as "making others happy makes us happy." The sixty-minute special featured simple songs about sharing, the wonder of imagination, being happy, the warm feeling of going home, the treasure of good friends. What's not to like? Barney is cuddly in toy-size, and a good teacher of ethical values in imagination-size.

All of the benefits notwithstanding, I'm not a fan of Barney. I find the metaphysical aspect of the show troublesome—the fact that Barney is a stuffed animal that comes to life as a walking, talking, miracle-working hero. In some ways, he is only one step removed from the shaman-like spirit-guide characters we find so readily prevalent on Saturday morning cartoons. He does what Jesus Christ *alone* can truly do in a person's life—give abiding comfort and be a source of divine love.

Children, in my opinion, should be encouraged to look to the living Lord for their guidance, joy, and comfort, not to their imaginations or toys. The Bible tells us that the unregenerated imagination of mankind is a fountain of evil (Genesis 6:5), and there's nothing about Barney that truly leads to a regenerated imagination.

My greater concern is that Barney is perceived as being a "good" show for children, and that many parents settle for good rather than pursuing the **best**. Barney is not the most creative or best produced children's show; neither is it the one with the best messages. In my opinion, *Salty* and the *Donut Man* series—both Christian in nature—are far more creative, engaging, and wholesome. Don't "settle" for Barney. Go for the true gold!

A Yabba Dabba Do Time . . .

Yabba dabba do!

That's the call of a program that features a different Barney, the one the **parents** of today's Barney's fans probably grew up with.

Virtually anybody who watched television in the 1960's no doubt can sing at least part of *The Flintstones* opening song, which promises viewers a "yabba dabba do time" in the city of Bedrock with Fred and Wilma Flintstone, Barney and Betty Rubble, and Fred's pet named "Dino" (pronounced DEE-no, for pre-Flintstone readers). The birth of the Flintstone's daughter, cute little Pebbles, was a national event!

The Flintstones lived simple, innocent lives. Fred worked in a quarry and had the usual troubles with boss and co-workers. Mostly, he and Barney got into trouble trying to cover up their own mistakes or "pull one over" on Wilma and Betty. In many ways, they were simply an animated take-off of *The Honeymooners* program, with a prehistoric spin.

Like their counterpart, *The Jetsons*, much of the visual intrigue and cleverness of the show involved the inventions, vehicles, and tools that the Flintstones and Rubbles used in their everyday lives.

In all, the Flintstones and Rubbles are characterized as sophisticated human beings, faced with the same temptations, struggles, problems, and joys of human beings today.

And Then There Are "The Dinosaurs"

Fred and Wilma Flintstone are nothing like Earl and Franny, today's "prehistoric" couple.

Beyond the obvious difference that Fred and Wilma are human characters and Earl and Franny are cast as dinosaurs with human traits and abilities, the dynamics of their home lives and the subject matter of the two shows are almost diametrically opposed.

It is beyond my understanding as to how this series could have been given the Parent's Choice Award. Still, with video boxes proclaiming that award, coupled with the fact that the video is distributed by Disney's Buena Vista subsidiary and that *Sesame Street* creator Jim Henson was involved in the puppetry, parents are likely to conclude that this show is fun family entertainment suitable for children. I heartily and emphatically disagree.

Here's just a sampling of the programs that have been aired, and that are now available in the video stores (packaged two episodes per cassette):

A Golden Child?

The episode called *The Golden Child* both opens and closes with the family watching the program "Ask Mr. Lizard" on their TV set. Twice, a child's head is blown off as part of an experiment and the prevailing line is, "We need another Timmy!" The family is shown enjoying and laughing along with this violent act.

The premise of this episode can be regarded as a spoof on the story of Christ's birth. The baby in the family experiences a major sugar high and shortly thereafter, grows a golden horn. According to the elders that meet in the Cave of Destiny in the Mountain of Terror, this golden horn qualifies the child to be king—as prophesied in the "Book of Dinosaur." Such a child was to have been born of a noble mother, is to be revered and worshipped, and is given absolute control over the kingdom. Adult dinosaurs are seen bowing down in worship of him.

Three of Earl's co-workers come to pay homage to Earl's son. They bring spices, silk, and a toy fire-truck.

A cloaked monk-like sage shows up magically and takes the child away so it can live with the elders. He lets the parents know that if they resist the child's going, they will be thrown into a fire.

In a clumsy act of showing homage to his son, Earl breaks off the golden horn and the child is deemed to be just an ordinary child who experienced something unexplained that "just happened."

As part of this particular episode, the father repeatedly points out that his life was easier when the family only had two children (the older Robbie and Charlene), and states his dismay at having a third child. In my opinion, that is not a message any child should hear coming from the mouth of any adult, even one portrayed as a ludicrous oaf.

Ethyl's Last Temptation

In the episode entitled "The Last Temptation of Ethyl"— obviously a take-off on the movie title *The Last Temptation of Christ*—a number of slams are taken against the Church and its teachings related to heaven.

Franny's mother, Ethyl, experiences an "out of body, near-death" experience as the result of choking on a potato chip. Son-in-law Earl proceeds to bury her, with some help from his TV-watching buddy, and without checking her pulse, getting a doctor's certification of death, or having a funeral. Earl and his pal joke about enjoying the burial process so much that they buried her fifteen feet deep rather than the customary six feet. The buddy comments that digging is good aerobic exercise, to which Earl responds, "Throwing your mother-in-law into a ditch is also a good pick-me-up." At another point in the segment, Earl refers to his mother-in-law as a parasite.

Upon her return to life, and after clawing her way out of her grave, Ethyl shares her afterlife experience with a "life's mysteries" TV program and is then contacted by a slick-and-slimey stereotype of a preacher who seeks her help in conducting his television ministry. As a focal point of "The Afterlife Show," Ethyl's experience is used, in the words of the thousand-member choir, to get viewers to "give dough to the Ethyl Show—give enough to carry you home." The pitch of the fund solicitation is to have viewers send money for condos and time-share places in the afterlife.

Ethyl describes the afterlife as a place with a monorail surrounding it, rides for all the kids, and no lines for the rides . . . and at another point in the program, says that it's a world with superb shopping opportunities: forty percent off and a great selection. She intimates that everybody goes there automatically, except for those who try to sell others on the idea of the afterlife.

The **idea** of an afterlife is openly stated to be a poor "alternative" to having real concern about current political and environmental issues. In a visit with her late husband, Ethyl hears him say that earth is more beautiful than the afterlife because earthly life is real **life.** The moral of the tale is to appreciate life and love others while you can—which Ethyl vows to do.

Switched Channels for Switched at Birth

The episode titled "Switched at Birth" opens with a beer commercial on DTV (Dinosaur TV). As Earl comes home, he gives his baby son a baseball bat. Franny comments, "You've got to earn his love," to which Earl replies, "I want it now—and I'm willing to pay for it." The baby hits his father with the baseball bat to the point of unconsciousness.

In cleaning out their cave, teenage daughter Charlene observes that Baby's "nest" has a different name on it. In meeting the other couple, they find a baby that looks more like them than their own—and that their Baby looks and acts more like the other couple. They undergo "scientific testing" and the conclusion is that the two eggs got switched just prior to their hatching. Franny is upset that her Baby is going to be exchanged and says to Earl, "If you let our Baby go out the door, I'll bite your face off." So much for spousal affection!

The two couples (and babies) consult a supposed "Solomon" character, in which magic is substituted for true wisdom. In the end, Baby returns to live with Earl and Franny and Solomon conjures up the scientist who explains that his tests were all in error.

The video box containing this episode advertises that this video includes "Baby's Funniest Adventures." I can't imagine a young child being amused by the idea that he or she might have been switched at birth, turned over to a strange couple, and cut into two in a magician's box!

This particular video also has the episode titled "Nature Calls." The episode deals with Baby's potty training. The show includes images of a potty chair being likened to an electric chair. The TV program the family watches includes a handgun murder.

In addition, the video has a "short" as an introduction— plugging Baby's video titled, "I'm the Baby." In it, Baby repeatedly hits his father (whom he calls "Not the Mama") with a frying pan and then a shovel. He also hits his mother and plugs his sister's tail into an electric socket.

Not funny, in my opinion.

Obnoxious and Undisciplined

Any way you look at him, the "baby" in this family is obnoxious and in many ways, diabolical.

Baby repeatedly talks back to his parents, refuses to obey them, hits them (usually hitting the father with a large saucepan), and has as his comment about any act of violence, danger, or general misbehavior, "Again!" Whenever an attempt is made to discipline the child, Baby responds, "I'm the baby. Gotta love me!" The net result is that Baby is *never* disciplined.

The show's characters are all stereotypes. Mother Franny is a stay-at-home monarch who cooks, cleans, and tries to get others to help (but never succeeds). Father Earl is portrayed as a blue-collar construction worker who is fat, lazy, not involved with his children, and likely to be found sitting in front of the TV set with a "brewskie." Teen son is into cheerleaders and being hip. Teen daughter Charlene is into shopping and fashion. Mother-in-law Ethyl is about as stereotypical a mother-in-law as one could find—a grouchy crab in a wheelchair who has little regard for anybody but herself and has an openly antagonistic relationship with her son-in-law.

In all, *Dinosaurs* is filled with crude talk, name-calling, very stereotypical figures, and promotes laughter at what normal people might consider to be important issues— juvenile delinquency among them.

A spoof on our culture? Yes, of course.

Good television? Well-directed and quality design.

A good message for children? No.

Elsewhere on Saturday Morning . . .

Cadillacs and Dinosaurs is a new CBS Saturday morning series set in the 26th century. Based on the comic book by the same title, the animated series features a young couple of ecologists who are cruising in an old Cadillac and find themselves in a prehistoric world. Again the images are fierce and the theme is one of fear, struggle, and human escape.

As a slight variation on the theme, the creators of Sesame Street have a new series out called *Cro*. It is an animated look at science and technology through the eyes of an eleven-year-old Cro-Magnon boy. Time travel in reverse!

In *Land of the Lost,* time travelers move through a "time porthole" that is created by an earthquake and find themselves in a prehistoric world. The program is aired on Saturday mornings and in some markets, as an after-school program. It has spun off a line of toys. For the most part, the dinosaur figures are fierce and demon-like. The travelers must engage in constant struggle against them to survive and danger lurks everywhere.

Prescreen and Watch Together

The best advice I can give you about children's television programming is to **watch it with your child.** When possible, or if you suspect that a program may have overtones, information, or violence you don't want you child to see, preview an episode by yourself. At other times, sit down to watch TV with your child. Talk about what you are seeing.

If at any time you find your child experiencing nightmares, an increase in sudden outbursts of anger, or continual imitating of violent behavior you know he has seen on television . . . turn off the programming and allow your child to turn on to his own imaginative play.

Young children *prefer* a gentle world. Our job is to provide one for them.

Guidelines for TV Viewing

Overall, I believe strongly that your children can make it just fine through life without ever watching a dinosaur of any variety on television! In fact, they'll be better off.

In our home, we limit "TV" viewing to four hours a week. Study after study has shown that persistence at task, analytical ability, and reading skills drop off dramatically among children who watch more than four hours of TV a week.

We have another policy regarding viewing: no television watching two days in a row. We don't want our children to "expect" television as part of their daily routine.

Very rarely do our children watch broadcast television; most of the programs they see are on video.

When our children do watch broadcast television, we watch the programs with them. One of the shows we enjoy as a family is *Rescue 911*. We talk with our children about the episodes and what should be done in our own home and lives should similar emergencies occur. We talk about the benefit of serving others in life-saving roles. We also talk about the commercials that air during the program and what the purpose of them is.

If our children don't watch broadcast television, what do they see? We probably have 250 videos in our family library— all of which we consider to be edifying or educational for our children, and none of which do we classify as "entertainment." We rent entertainment videos; we buy education and faith-building videos.

"Well," you may say, "if your videos are educational and faith-building, why not allow your children to watch more?" In part, because we don't want our children to become reliant on television as their source of information or inspiration. We prefer to see them learn from books, encounters with other people, and from self-motivated and creative play.

The Apostle Paul taught that our faith is not to become reliant upon *the wisdom of men but in the power of God* (1 Corinthians 2:5). We know this power when we commune with the Lord and as we engage in His will and service to others. We *don't* know His power through watching a program on a television monitor, no matter how fine the program.

Television is enticing. It moves. It attracts. It preys upon the emotions. It presents much that we would objectively call evil and detrimental to our society. It "sells." In sum, it encourages a good many people to bow down and worship other gods. We must guard against its influence, and part of that includes guarding against its overuse in our lives and its "over-play" in the lives of our children.

Many parents seem to opt for the "video flavor of the month." They rent or buy a video and allow their children to be entertained by it over and over and over and over. As far as I'm concerned, that's tantamount to a parent placing a giant bowl of M&M's in the middle of the dinner table at each meal and then "hoping" that their children will develop healthy eating habits and enjoy sound nutrition. We must choose what our children emotionally and spiritually consume. We must make sure that they encounter food that is not only healthful, but in balanced proportion. Just as sweets should probably amount to no more than five percent of a child's diet, so we believe that our children's spiritual diet should include no more than five percent entertainment.

Part of the control of television use in our family is a matter of self-control and obedience. We want our children to be able to self-regulate their own appetites for what our culture has to offer. We trust that if they develop that ability regarding television at an early age, they'll have that ability when it comes to saying "no" to certain enticements of the culture later.

There's very little about dinosaurs on television that is worthy of a "yes."

12

Dinosaurs on the Shelves and in the Toy Box

New dinosaur books are being released all the time. Here is a smattering of what's out there today. For the most part, it's not a pretty sight.

The problem with most dinosaur books for children is that they present evolution as a fact.

Consider, as an example, *The Big Golden Book of Dinosaurs* (published in 1988 as A Golden Book, by Western Publishing Company, Inc.). This book, with about sixty pages of exposition about different types of dinosaurs, concludes with four pages of explanation about the world "After the Dinosaurs."

In describing the world of mammals the book says, "At first the mammals were too small to make much noise, but after a while new and larger ones began to appear. Then some of them died out, and different ones developed. This happened again and again."

The explanation continues, "One especially important group of mammals was the primates—our own ancestors. Fossil bones, very much like our bones, have been found in rocks that are more than three million years old. But scientists are not sure just when true human beings

173

first appeared. Perhaps we will never know exactly when people began to talk and sing and wonder about things. It must have happened when brains grew bigger and developed a complicated top part—the part sometimes called the "thinking cap." The illustrations on this two-page spread include those of two apes: *Dryopithecus* (identified as a Miocene ape), and *Australopithecine*, which has this identifier: "possible Homo sapiens ancestor."

Aliki has written and illustrated a number of nonfiction books about dinosaurs for children. Among them are *Digging Up Dinosaurs*, *My Visit to the Dinosaurs*, *Dinosaur Bones,* and *Dinosaurs Are Differerent*. The books have lots of factual information and color drawings, and they are very popular with librarians . . . but Christian parents need to be aware that they present the evolutionist line of thought.

Dinotopia, a book by James Gurney, has carefully painted illustrations that are based on fact as far as we know them. But the story is pure imagination. His story is about an island where dinosaurs have survived—an island on which, over the years, human beings are shipwrecked. Man and dinosaur live in great harmony.

One of the most thorough and interesting books on the market is called *Dinosaur and Other Prehistoric Animal Fact Finder* by Michael Benton. The book is well-organized and has an A-to-Z list of more than 200 dinosaurs and prehistoric animals, good clear pictures, and rather long descriptions of each creature. Maps show where particular dinosaur remains have been found in the world and illustrations show how big each dinosaur was compared to a man, where it lived, when, and by whom its remains were first discovered. (Again, it assumes a multi-million-year past.)

Macmillan's Children's Guide to Dinosaurs and *Dinosaur and Other Prehistoric Animal Fact Finder* are popular resources that describe facts about dinosaurs.

Jurassic Park Spin-Off Books

The Making of Jurassic Park is an impressive book, indeed. The book covers pre-production, production, post-production, and gives samples of story boards and a complete listing of film credits. Just as the movie is not for children, neither is this book. It's really a teen or adult book.

The movie was turned into a four-issue comic-book series with some of the biggest names in the comic-book world doing the script, pencils, and inks: Watler Simonson, Gil Kane, and George Perez. Trading cards were offered with each issue.

A more tongue-in-cheek "Mad-Magazine-style" approach was taken by a comic-book titled "Cracked." The character Barney is also parodied in the comic book, as a chomping, crunching child-eater who proclaims, "What do ya expect? I *am* a Tyrannosaurus, you know!" Both thumbs down on this one.

Comics Are Definitely Dinosaur Territory

Marvel has put out a series of books called "Dinosaurs—A Celebration." The series includes such titles as "Terrible Claws and Tyrants," "Bone-Heads and Duck-Bills," and "Horns and Heavy Armor." The books combine facts, diagrams, and full-color illustrations related to dinosaurs, which are interspersed with comic-book-style panels of action.

A series of dinosaur comic books are being published by Malibu comics. The dinosaurs are cops but the comic books are lewd, crude, and violent.

Dinosaurs were popular in the comics even before there were comic books. The early adventure strips such as *Alley Oop, Tarzan, Brick Bradford* and *Flash Gordon* regularly featured a *Tyrannosaurus* on the Sunday pages.

One of the great appeals, of course, is that dinosaurs look so different. There are only so many variations to the average monster—add an eye or a fang, a scale or a feather—but with dinosaurs, the differences are numerous. On the downside, from an artist's perspective, is that dinosaurs offer little color variation—mostly dull browns and greens.

It's a little surprising to think that dinosaurs didn't star in their own comic book lines before 1978, with *Tor and Turok, Son of Stone. Tor*, regarded now as a classic, is pretty much the caveman versus dinosaur story. Both were to be rereleased in the wake of *Jurassic Park*.

Up to that time, dinosaurs were something of "guest stars" in series such as DC's *Rip Hunter, Time Master*. Most of the story lines included time travel.

A Marvel series published in 1978 by comics giant Jack Kirby was called *Devil Dinosaur*. The series had only nine issues, but someone apparently paid attention to "number eight" D a story called "Dino Riders." A few years later that title became its own series title, and also spun off an animated television series for children.

Dinosaurs as Attention Getters

Finally, there are a number of books that feature dinosaurs, but which aren't about dinosaurs at all. Publishers have joined in the manufacturing approach to using dinosaurs as a theme simply to attract and hold a child's attention.

Take for example, a little book titled "Time for School, Little Dinosaur." It's one of a series of Pictureback Readers—books told with fifty or fewer words designed especially for young readers—published by Random House.

Little Dinosaur sleeps in a bed, packs a lunch pail, and waits for a school bus—none of which are activities even remotely befitting a true dinosaur! Little Dinosaur is the "model child," as opposed to a character named Spikey who fails to pack his book bag and lunch and nearly misses the bus on the first day of school (and would have, except for Little Dinosaur's help).

Little Dinosaur could just as easily have been a child figure—except the publishers apparently thought a cute, roundly-drawn green *Stegosaurus* would make an appealing figure for children.

Dinosaurs are Roaring in the Toy Stores

The toy market, as might easily be concluded, has been quick to jump on the dinosaur band wagon created by *Jurassic Park*. For that matter, *Jurassic Park* was never intended to be just a book or just a movie. In the words of MCA/Universal Merchandising President Sid Kaufman, speaking at a new conference at the American International Toy Fair: "*Jurassic Park* is . . . a merchandising and marketing opportunity."

Even before the movie was released, MCA had sold more than 100 licenses for 1,000 products which were expected to generate more than $100 million in revenues.

Toy buyers can expect to see video games for Sega and Nintendo systems, as well as board games and model kits.

A video game version of *Jurassic Park* is being designed for 3DO Company—3DO being the format that many are calling the next generation of videogame systems.

The hottest toy product in 1993 was expected to be Kenner's Jurassic Park. The line includes people figures and dinosaur figures (in the $6-7 range), an electronic *Tyrannosaurus rex* (in the $30-40 range), and a "Command Compound Play Set" ($50-60).

In looking at all 1993 licenses, Jurassic Park seems to be the runaway leader for 1993 . . . and Barney is number two!

Barney's a Toy, Too

Barney's videotapes and plush toys seem to have been selling the best of all Barney products.

The world's largest toy manufacturer, Hasbro Inc., recently signed a licensing agreement to feature Barney. The Hasbro line will include interactive toys, puzzles, games, and baby products featuring Barney and his friend Baby Bop. Under a cross-licensing agreement, five Hasbro divisions—Playskool, Playskool Baby, Parker Brothers, Kid Dimension, and Milton Bradley—will have Barney-related products.

Parker Brothers has come out with "Sounds of Fun, " an electronic talking board game with the voices of Barney, Baby Bop, and other sound effects. In Picture Game, players travel through Barney's neighborhood collecting pictures of him. The Jumbo Card Game has children forming pairs of Barney and Baby Bop.

Playskool toys include a Talking Barney. Just squeeze his hand and you'll hear lines like "Let's walk like a duck!" Rub his tummy and he gives one of 500 "loving phrases." In the Kid Dimension line are vinyl Barney and Baby Bop figures in various outfits and poses.

For very young children (ages 6 months to 3 years), Bounce-Back is a soft inflatable Barney that jingles when it is thrown. The toy "rolls back" when pushed away. Tumble Wheel has Barney and Baby Bop presenting the alphabet on a soft, durable inflatable tube. Peek 'N Play is an inflatable tube with jingling balls.

Even before the current wave of dinosaur mania, Hasbro introduced "Baby Sinclair"—a talking dinosaur doll that sold-out in a national chain at a price of $34.94 per unit. Smaller dinosaur figures priced at $4 and $5 were nearly as popular. The doll was adapted from an ABC-TV series.

Dinosaur "trading cards" have appeared in a number of forms—some of them portraying "scenes," while others present facts related to a particular species. There's even a company in California called "Dinocardz."

New-Ray Toys has a line of wind-up dinosaur toys.

Tiger Electronics Inc. packaged its *Land of the Lost* dinosaur-themes characters with a "genuine fossil" labeled as being from the Jurassic Period (140 million years ago).

DaMert Co., a small science and nature specialty company, used a red-eyed *Tyrannosaurus rex* on the cover of its catalog. Products offered included a dinosaur puzzle and holographic dinosaur stickers.

The Little Tikes Co., a division of Rubbermaid, offered a purple and yellow sandbox-swimming pool combination in the shape of what was called a "friendly dinosaur."

Tyco's "Dino Riders" were among the best-selling action figure dolls in the 1980's. They're still on the market.

Dinosaurs for Girls

A number of new dinosaur products, interestingly, are targeted for girls.

Meritus Industries has introduced a line of dinosaur dolls. Called "Darlin' Dinos," these brightly colored dinosaurs have the names of Bronte, the swamp sweetheart; T-Rexanne, the *pterosaur*, and Tri-Sarah Tops. The dinosaur dolls have long hair for combing and styling. A similar product called "Gemdazzlers" comes in six colors, each with a styling comb.

"Lil' Dinos" are colorful, two-inch miniatures. "Bendables" are dinosaurs that are pliable enough to wrap around a girl's hand.

"Sweet Talkers" wear a jewel on their chests, which, when pushed, says "I'm so cute" followed by a roar. "Snazzies" are dinosaur figures in special attire: Snorkel Diver has a scuba mask, snorkel, and flippers, Fancy Dancer has a fruit bowl hat and maracas, Cowgirl has a hat and hobby horse, and In-Line Skater has skates and a helmet.

"Dressy Dinos" are a bride, doctor, princess, birthday girl, or baseball player. "Dino Stuffs" are plush dinos in pink, blue, purple, and green. "Hug 'n' Hold Dino" is a large, machine washable doll with jewels, long hair, and a host of accessories: rings, pencil toppers, belt bags, backpacks, and pocketbooks."

For Imagination, Not Emulation

In purchasing dinosaur "dolls" and toys for your child, ask yourself a key question:

How will my child play with this?

If the toy is linked to an action-oriented television series, your child will likely give characterizations and plots to the toy that he or she has already seen on TV. That's not good play. Good play is imaginative—play in which your child "makes up" plots, characters, and dialog.

Also ask yourself: Is my child interested in this solely because it is a dinosaur? If so, the toy probably has limited value. As with all toys, make sure that the toy is safe . . . makes lots of "play hours" possible . . . and is within the age range suitable for your child.

13

Why Now?

Why all of the interest in dinosaurs these days? All things considered, men and women, boys and girls have been fascinated by the idea of giant terrible lizards and a prehistoric age for the last one 175 years, since the first fossilized bones were identified. Perhaps the greater questions are these:

Why has the Lord waited until now to reveal the *fullness* of His creation?

Why was dinosaur evidence preserved for thousands of years, and only recently made known to mankind?

Counterfeits Precede the Truth in Many Cases

There are a number of speculations we can make about why God may have waited until just "recently" (in terms of history's timetable) to tell us about dinosaurs, but perhaps these are the foremost ideas supported by the Bible's teachings.

First, *it seems that throughout history, the devil has made an attempt to pre-empt God's plan just prior to the time when God's plan is fully revealed.*

The enemy puts out a "counterfeit truth" or a "diversionary approach" in an attempt to draw people away from the truth, and to close their minds so that when the truth is presented to them, they have "already made up their minds" in a different direction.

The Bible tells us clearly that Satan is the father of all lies. He is the original deceiver and counterfeiter. His goal is to woo as many people as possible away from God's truth. (See John 8:44.)

The Bible also tells us in John 10:10 that the devil's tactics are to steal, kill, and destroy. There is nothing **good** about the devil's plan for us individually, or as a body of humanity. The devil's lies always lead to our destruction, or to the destruction of other people.

I could point to a number of counterfeit philosophies and opinions that have appeared throughout history, but perhaps two in very recent history within our own nation can serve to illustrate the point.

In the 1970's, the science of genetics really began to take off. Today, we are quite accustomed to terms such as DNA marking, gene pools (especially as they relate to disease), genetic engineering, the splicing of genes, the word "clone," and perhaps the next wave in medical treatment: "gene therapy." Prior to 1970, those terms were not a part of the common vocabulary in our nation.

What happened just prior to that upsurge in genetic research and interest? A lie was infused into the American culture. We began to talk about pre-born babies as "fetuses." A child in the womb literally was described as "a blob of tissue," subject to the control of the woman who hosted it in her body. The decision to terminate a pregnancy was not seen as the killing of a human being, but as a legal right to abort, which for the most part, was perceived to be the "end of a problem."

Today, most attorneys and scientists agree that the *scientific* evidence is such that Roe v. Wade would never have become the standard allowing for legalized abortion. In the first place, science could far better argue today that a human being is independent *genetically* in its identity from the first division of cells in the mother's womb. The issue of "viability" is vastly different today than thirty years ago. (In vitro fertilization is but one example of life multiplying and forming outside the womb—life with a distinctively human imprint and genetic code.) The understanding of fetal development is far more precise. Women today routinely have sonograms that show them the living being inside their wombs—a technique that didn't exist when abortion became legal. Still, by the time genetic research and science caught up with the legal and political opinion of the day, the die had been cast. Truth began to play "catch up" to the lie about life's origin that had already been swallowed, for the most part, by the vast majority of the population.

We must never forget that it is much more difficult to refute a lie or overturn a lie than it is to tell a lie.

Another case in counterfeit theorizing might be the issue of prayer.

We are just now beginning to learn more about how prayer works. An area of medicine is truly being pioneered today to integrate prayer with the healing process. Studies are being done that link prayer to medical care, recovery from surgery, and the improvement of psychological conditions.

More and more churches are initiating prayer ministries and establishing prayer teams. In my evangelistic travels across this nation during the last fifteen years, I've seen a dramatic increase in the number of "prayer groups" that have arisen within the Church. Specific houses of prayer, prayer centers, prayer towers, prayer hotlines, and prayer mountains have been established—all in the last 25 years. We are in the midst of a great prayer wave and more and more is being written about how prayer works, what types of prayer seem effective for specific troubles, and so forth. In many ways, we are just beginning to learn how prayer works—at least on a broad-based scale within the Body of Christ.

Many church historians mark this new era of prayer as really taking off in the 1960's, as part of the great outpouring of the Holy Spirit upon God's people in mainline denominations.

The counterfeit, diversionary move? Prayer was eliminated from our public schools on the grounds that it was politically inappropriate (supposedly owing to our Constitutional standard separating Church and state), unnecessary, and divisive. Again, the truth is playing tag now with a lie.

But back to dinosaurs . . .

In my opinion, the enemy's counterfeit maneuver on the issue of dinosaurs happened in the middle 1800's with the rise of Darwinian theory and the establishment of evolution as the "modern" approach to the origin of all species. It may be difficult for many people to realize that it is so . . . but "evolution" is very new on the scene of human thought. It didn't exist as a theory 150 years ago. It was a "new idea," spawned in the period called "enlightened" (a decidedly unChristian, antiBible era of thought).

At the time Darwin's theory began to be popularized—and in many ways, twisted from his original thinking and writing, although the warped ideas were still attributed to his name and theory—ninety-nine plus percent of the dinosaur bones we have today had not been discovered! The sedimentary layers of the earth's crust were the cornerstone of the theory. Most of what was proposed was postured as an **idea**, intended to prompt discussion and research, although there was actually little hope at the time of finding evidence that could fully substantiate the theory's main points.

Why this as a *diversionary* tactic? This leads us to a second major point related to dinosaur research and interest.

"Beginning Error" Is Also "Ending Error"

Second, *dinosaurs deal with the beginning of God's creation. They are creatures that belong to the earth in a form that we do not experience today.*

If the enemy can divert our thinking away from the truth about the Bible's account of creation and the way things began . . . then it's only one small step to the point where the enemy can also divert our thinking away from the truth about the way things will **end!**

The Bible clearly states that the earth as we know it today will **end.** That end is described as being a dramatic, earth-changing event that Christians around the world call "The Second Coming"—the return of Jesus Christ, our Lord, to this earth in order to establish His reign over the nations.

Evolutionary science tells us that the development of life happened slowly . . . cell by cell . . . creature by creature . . . species by species . . . over millions and millions— yes, even *hundreds* of millions of years. In evolution, time passes slowly. Decisions happen gradually. And above all, life changes *accidentally.*

- In **evolution** there is no comprehensive divine plan.
- In **evolution** there is no concept of divine judgment.
- In **evolution** there is no foreseeable end to life as we know it—only gradual change, and that to the point of happening so slowly as to be virtually imperceptible.

What a grand lie to have in place even as the whole church seems to be waiting on tiptoe these days for the return of the Lord Jesus!

The Bible says that when Jesus returns, we will experience a "new heaven and a new earth." A new order will be established in which all the nations of the earth are subject to Jesus, the King of kings and Lord of lords. Bible scholars for decades have envisioned a new earth that is actually very much like the original creation—an earth in which people live a thousand years and life is in perfect balance without the influence of sin, death, or violence.

Just as the old earth was renovated by a flood of judgment, so the earth we live in presently will be renovated and a new creative order—or dispensation, in theological terms—will be put into effect.

Those who buy into evolution will not only be unprepared for such an event, the very idea of it will seem preposterous to them.

What is the net result?

The final result of the enemy's ploy is to discount God's plan and in the process, leave individuals:

- without the hope of His return,
- unprepared for His return,
- blinded to the spiritual significance of events that are unfolding rapidly all around us,
- and without a deep sense of need for a Savior, Redeemer, Deliverer.

The final result is . . . people with souls unredeemed and lives lived unaware of God's great love for them and His divine plan for their fulfillment.

14

What Should We Do?
What position should we take?
What action should we pursue?

Here are eight things I believe strongly that every Christian parent should do:

First, *arm your child with Bible-related facts about dinosaurs.* Talk to your child about Creation and the Great Flood. Provide books, movies, videos, audio tapes, and activity books that provide children with dinosaur materials that tell the truth about dinosaurs and history—not the distorted evolutionary theories. In addition to sources previously recommended, I've added a list of books and videos at the end of this chapter.

Second, *talk to your children about the Creator who gave these creatures their life. What do the dinosaurs tell us about the immense variety and power of God's creativity?*

Encourage your child's interest in God's creation. Emphasize these points:

- God has a *fantastic* imagination! The wonders of the natural world are truly amazing, astounding, and awesome! Ephesians 3:20 tells us that the Lord is "able to do exceedingly abundantly above all that we ask or think." Encourage your child to view the Lord as the One who has unlimited power, ability,and creativity.

187

- Point out to your child that God initially told Adam, and then repeated the command to Noah, that man was to have "dominion" over all the animals. This word "dominion" does not only mean power and authority, but full "understanding" about the animals. We are *supposed* to know as much as possible about God's creatures in order to learn from them and to take care of them, and to begin to understand just how God designed His creation to work in harmony.

- Discuss with your child ways in which the Lord asks us today to be the stewards of the earth—to care for the plants and animals. This does not mean, as some are teaching our children, that we are not to use animals for food or for such important work as medical research. God told Noah that the animals were his both to eat and to harness (or to put touseful work). It does mean that we are not to waste God's creation, to torture it or abuse it, or to fail to replenish and restore that which we take for our use. Talk openly with your child about extinction and the wisdom of keeping species alive.

Don't dissuade or discourage your child's interest in dinosaurs, any more than you would discourage his or her interest in any other aspect of God's creation. This world needs more Christians involved in scientific research so that we might unlock the mysteries that God has for us to discover in the study of plants, mammals, reptiles, fish, birds, and even early-earth or extinct species.

Third, *prescreen as many of the materials that your child will encounter as you are able.* Look for strains of teaching about evolution. Talk to your child about what he is reading or seeing.

Fourth, *if you don't have the opportunity to prescreen materials, be sure that you watch movies and videos about dinosaurs with your child, and that you read books with your* *child whenever possible.* Of course, this is not only a good monitoring technique, but also a good emotional bonding technique with your child!

Fifth, *tell your child about evolution.* Don't wait for the schools to do it.

Children should know about evolution and what it teaches. This is not to say that they should be taught to **believe** evolution, but they should be familiar with evolution as a theory and know its tenets. At the same time, they need to be taught what creation science teaches and how the two theories relate (or don't relate).

A child should know that evolution is rooted in a **belief** system, just as all theories eventually have a belief system or a philosophical orientation driving them.

Evolution is based upon the belief that organisms change over time to become different (both morphologically and physiologically—or in simply terms, both in their appearance and the way their bodies function).

Make sure you use the correct terminology. Here are basic words you need to know:

- *Evolutionism* is the acceptance of the theory of biological evolution, especially as that theory was formulated by Charles Darwin.

- *Evolution science* is the study of **how** evolution happens. It is an attempt, using the scientific method, to find evidence to support the theory of evolution.

- *Creation* is frequently referred to as The Creation. When used in that manner, it refers to God's primal act of bringing the world into existence. When used in a more general sense, the word refers to the producing of an original work.

- *Creationism* is the doctrine that says the *origin* of all matter and living forms as they presently exist is the result of distinct acts of God.

189

- *Creation science* is the attempt to prove, using the scientific method, that The Creation account of the Bible is a viable scientific theory.

If your child is not enrolled in public school—where you will find a lot of information about evolution in your child's textbooks . . . .

You can find information about dinosaurs and evolution in basic encyclopedias and even dictionaries. The "Geologic Column" or "Geologic Time Scale" is presented in most dictionaries.

Don't just tell your child that evolution is wrong or bad . . . point out to them precisely what evolution teaches and why you believe that approach is in error! Arm your child with facts and figures, not only opinions.

Sixth, *donate creationist books to libraries— especially to Christian school libraries and church libraries.*

Seventh, *push for inclusion of dinosaurs in story-telling and vacation-Bible-school programs that talk about creation, Noah and the ark, and other early Genesis stories.* The last place many children hear about dinosaurs is in church. It should be one of the first places they hear about them!

Eighth, *if your child is in public school, monitor his textbooks and homework papers closely.* Take an active interest in what is being taught to your child.

Take heart! We know more about science and about the Bible today than ever in history.

Evolution theory is in more disrepute and under greater threat of "extinction" now than in just about any time during the last one hundred years.

Creation science is developing rapidly and experiments based on its position are being conducted regularly now.

The truth *will* win out.

A Personal Note From the Author

Now that you have read this book . . . .

For over eleven years I have been fighting for your children, and millions of parents, grandparents, pastors and teachers have been influenced by this ministry. Although my ministry may be new to you, much of the increased awareness we see today on the affect of toys and media on children are fruit from the seed I planted as a young man.

At age four I gave my heart to the Lord, and at age fifteen I was called into the ministry. I have never strayed from that calling and have always considered it an honor and privilege to serve the Lord in full-time ministry.

My wife Cynthia serves in the ministry with me as well as home schools our four children. We have dedicated our lives to confronting issues that affect children and challenging parents to train and command their children.

One of my most recent books, *Helping Your Children Walk With God,* reveals the heart of this ministry. It is one of the most important books I have ever written and every parent and grandparent who desires that their children know God in a deeper way needs this book.

This 260 page book is available for your donation of any size to our ministry. Please make your checks payable to Child Affects. Send to Child Affects, P.O. Box 68, Rockwall, Texas 75087. Your gift is tax deductible.

Thank you in advance for your generous donation to help me continue this fight for your children.

For the Children,
Phil Phillips

Phil Phillips is available for speaking engagements, parent training workshops and interviews. If your church or organization is interested in scheduling Phil Phillips write to:

Child Affects
Phil Phillips, Director
P.O. Box 68
Rockwall, Texas 75087
Telephone (817) 430-1774

A Recommended Reading and Viewing List

For young readers:

- Unfred, David, *Dinosaurs and the Bible*, Huntington House Publishers, P. O. Box 53788, Lafayette, Louisiana 70505 (1990).

- Taylor, Paul S., *The Great Dinosaur Mystery and the Bible*, Master Books, CLP, Inc., P. O. Box 1606, El Cajon, California 92022 (1953). (Taylor is also the screenwriter of a movie entitled, *The Great Dinosaur Mystery.*)

For teen readers and adults:

- Baugh, Carl E., Ph.D., *Dinosaur—Scientific Evidence That Dinosaurs and Men Walked Together*, Creation Evidence Museum, P. O. Box 309, Glen Rose, Texas 76043. Telephone (817) 897-3200. (A video is also available.)

For adults, books giving a Christian approach to science and evolution:

- Anderson, Bernard W., *Creation in the Old Testament*
- Cupitti, Don, *Creation Out of Nothing*
- Drane, John, *The Bible: Fact or Fantasy?*
- Faid, Robert W., *A Scientific Approach to Biblical Mysteries*
- Faid, Robert W., *A Scientific Approach to Christianity*
- Johnson, Phillip E., *Darwin on Trial*
- Matrisciana, Caryl and Roger Oakland, *The Evolution Conspiracy*
- Morris, Henry M., *Science and the Bible*
- Morris, Henry M., *The Remarkable Record of Job*
- Morris, Henry M., *Evolution and the Modern Christian*
- Morris, Henry M., *The Biblical Basis for Modern Science*
- Morris, Henry M., *The Genesis Record*
- Morris, Henry M., *The Long War Against God*

You'll notice the name Henry M. Morris several times on the preceding page. For a full catalog of materials published by his institute call:

The Institute for Creation Research
(619) 448-0900

Roger Oakland is a well-known lecturer, author, and former biology teacher whose name is also listed on the preceding page. You can write for a full list of the materials he has available at:

Oakland Communications
P. O. Box 27239
Santa Ana, CA 92799

The Truth About Dungeons & Dragons   —Joan Hake Robie

A close look at the fascinating yet dangerous game of Dungeons and Dragons. What it is about. Why it holds such fascination for certain people, especially young, well-educated and gifted people.

(trade paper)   ISBN 0914984373   **$5.95**
(audio cassette)   ISBN 091498425X   **$7.95**

Teenage Mutant Ninja Turtles Exposed!   —Joan Hake Robie

Looks closely at the national popularity of Teenage Mutant Ninja Turtles. Tells what they teach and how this "turtle" philosophy affects children (and adults) mentally, emotionally, socially, morally, and spiritually. The book gives the answer to what we can do about the problem.

(trade paper)   ISBN 0914984314   **$5.95**

Beyond The River   —Gilbert Morris & Bobby Funderburk

The first novel of *The Far Fields* series, **Beyond the River** makes for intriguing reading with high spiritual warfare impact. Set in the future and in the mode of *Brave New World* and *1984,* **Beyond The River** presents a world that is ruined by modern social and spiritual trends. This anti-utopian novel offers an excellent opportunity to speak to the issues of the New Age and "politically-correct" doctrines that are sweeping the country.

(trade paper)   ISBN 0914984519   **$8.95**

A Woman's Guide To Spiritual Power   —Nancy L. Dorner

Subtitled: *Through Scriptural Prayer.* Do your prayers seem to go "against a brick wall?" Does God sometimes seem far away or non-existent? If your answer is "Yes," *You* are not alone. Prayer must be the cornerstone of your relationship to God. "This book is a powerful tool for anyone who is serious about prayer and discipleship."—Florence Littauer

(trade paper)   ISBN 0914984470   **$9.95**

The World's Oldest Health Plan   —Kathleen O'Bannon Baldinger

Subtitled: *Health, Nutrition and Healing from the Bible.* Offers a complete health plan for body, mind and spirit, just as Jesus did. It includes programs for diet, exercise and mental health. Contains foods and recipes to lower cholesterol and blood pressure, improve the immune system and other bodily functions, reduce stress, reduce or cure constipation, eliminate insomnia, reduce forgetfulness, confusion and anger, increase circulation and thinking ability, eliminate "yeast" problems, improve digestion, and much more.

(trade paper-opens flat)   ISBN 0914984578   **$14.95**

On The Brink — Daymond R. Duck

Subtitled: *Easy-to-Understand End-Time Bible Prphecy.* Organized in Biblical sequence and written with simplicity so that any reader will easily understand end-time prophecy. Ideal for use as a handy-reference book.

(trade paper) ISBN 0-914984-586 **$9.95**

The Beast Of The East — Alvin M. Shifflett

Asks the questions: Has the Church become involved in a "late date" comfort mode—expecting to be "raptured" before the Scuds fall? Should we prepare for a long and arduous Desert Storm to Armageddon battle? Are we ignoring John 16:33, *In this world you will have trouble?* (NIV)

(trade paper) ISBN 0914984411 **$6.95**

Political Correctness Exposed — Marvin Sprouse

Subtitled—*A Piranha in Your Bathtub.* Explores the history of Political Correctness, how it originated, who keeps it alive today, and more importantly, how to combat Political Correctness. Contains 25 of the most frequently told Politically Correct lies.

(trade paper) ISBN 0914984624 **$9.95**

Purchasing Information

Listed books are available from your favorite Bookstore, either from current stock or special order. To assist bookstore in locating your selection be sure to give title, author, and ISBN #. If unable to purchase from the bookstore you may order direct from STARBURST PUBLISHERS. When ordering enclose full payment plus $2.50* for shipping and handling ($3.00* if Canada or Overseas). Payment in US Funds only. Please allow two to three weeks minimum (longer overseas) for delivery. Make checks payable to and mail to STARBURST PUBLISHERS, P.O. Box 4123, LANCASTER, PA 17604. **Prices subject to change without notice**. Catalog available upon request.

*We reserve the right to ship your order the least expensive way. If you desire first class (domestic) or air shipment (Canada) please enclose shipping funds as follows: First Class within the USA enclose $4.50, Airmail Canada enclose $6.00.   10-94